LISTEN TO WHAT PEOPLE ARE ALREADY SAYING ABOUT *HOLDING ON TO HOPE*

You hold in your hand a treasure that was mined
in a dark and frightening place. With transparent honesty,
Nancy unwraps the joys and sorrows of her life. This
is a book about life and our God, who holds us in
all the moments of this life.

SHEILA WALSH
keynote speaker with Women of Faith

Holding on to Hope reads easy, runs deep, and enriches
the heart! If you are stymied about God's goodness
amidst life's heartaches, then this book's for you.

JONI EARECKSON TADA
Joni and Friends

Few people have lived—and continue to live—as deep
a firsthand experience of pain and loss as Nancy Guthrie.
For that reason alone her Christian reading of the story
of Job should lay special claim on readers themselves
undergoing suffering. But there are other inducements:
the clarity, grit, and honesty with which Guthrie explains
how she has maintained hope and deepened faith
where most would find only heartbreak.

DAVID VAN BIEMA
Time magazine

Only God could orchestrate such events. And only God
could give the Guthrie family the faith and courage to live
them. May He use this story to strengthen us all.

MAX LUCADO

Nancy Guthrie's faith shines through some of the darkest clouds of human pain. This book and her story will touch your emotions and inspire your mind in an unforgettable way. Seldom will you read anything with such candor and insight, probing one of life's toughest questions: How can grief be a friend along life's journey?

RAVI ZACHARIAS

HOLDING ON TO HOPE

A *pathway through suffering to the heart of God*

NANCY GUTHRIE

Tyndale House Publishers, Inc.
Wheaton, Illinois

Visit Tyndale's exciting Web site at www.tyndale.com

Author photo by Micael-Reneé.

Hope Guthrie photo by Micael-Reneé.

Gabriel Guthrie photo by Micael-Reneé.

Edited by Lisa A. Jackson

Designed by Zandrah Maguigad

ISBN 1-4143-0126-x

Printed in the United States of America

09 08 07 06 05 04
7   6   5   4   3   2   1

CONTENTS

FOREWORD

By Anne Graham Lotz

On September 11, 2001, terrorists hijacked four airliners, ramming two of the planes into the twin towers of the World Trade Center in New York City. The entire world watched in horror as the towers erupted into gigantic fireballs, then imploded until nothing was left of the 110-story, glass-and-steel structures except soot, dust, and a six-story-high pile of smoldering rubble.

Even before the dust settled, the heroic rescue effort began as thousands of people systematically started combing through the debris to find the survivors. One rescuer told how he had climbed down into a hole in the twisted steel and rubble, extending his arm even farther to shine his flashlight into the darkness, when out of the dusty blackness a hand reached up and grabbed his! He was so startled he almost dropped his flashlight and let go of the hand! But instead, he reached back for someone to grab his hand, then someone grabbed that person's hand, until a human chain was formed and the man trapped in the pile of debris was pulled to safety.

In our world today, there are many people who are trapped in the debris of despair, depression, and doubt; or in the rubble of broken relationships; or in the twisted maze of suffering and pain. God has uniquely equipped Nancy Guthrie as a "rescuer" to shine the light of God's truth into the blackest night of confusion and grief, hopelessness and helplessness. Framing the testimony of her own suffering within the classic biblical story of Job, Nancy draws a magnificent picture of triumphant victory through faith in Jesus Christ.

In a world where so much attention has been focused on a Christian message of health, wealth, and prosperity, *Holding on to Hope* is like a beacon of Light, drawing the reader to God and God alone.

My prayer is that God will use this book to rescue you from the depths of being buried alive in the debris and rubble of your own life experience. And I pray also that your feet will be planted on the solid ground of his Word, setting your spirit free to soar in the rarefied atmosphere of genuine worship. God bless you as you grasp Nancy's hand and allow her to guide you on your own path of suffering that leads to the heart of God.

ACKNOWLEDGMENTS
Thank You

To Anne Graham Lotz, who helped me see God's perspective. It *was* a very important mission. Thank you for walking through it with me.

To Ernie and Pauline Owen, who see me through rose-colored glasses and never cease to believe in me.

To Dan and Sue Johnson, for taking the time to care so deeply and for helping us to find the answers to the questions.

To all those who so faithfully and unselfishly served me—Mary Grace, Mary Bess, Joanna, Julie, Gigi, Lori, Jan, Angela, and the Coates women, to name a few. I'm forever bankrupt to repay you.

To Allen Arnold, for giving me so much time and input, and for wanting to buy the first copy.

To everyone in the Knox group, and to Jana and Pamela, for giving them a voice.

To Mom, Dad, Rita, and Wink, who suffered doubly by losing their granddaughter and watching their daughter and son lose a daughter. You are the world's best grandparents.

To the Group: Buchanans, Davises, Hodges, MacKenzies, Baughers, Blackburns, Yarboroughs, Pfaehlers, and, of course, the glue that holds us together—Evelyn. Thanks for laughing with us and crying with us and meeting our needs before we knew we had them.

To Matt, for giving me such a good reason to keep getting up in the morning.

And especially to David. I guess we had more in common than we even knew. Thank you for letting me make our pain so public. She *was* beautiful, wasn't she?

HOPE IS SYMBOLIZED in Christian iconography by an anchor. And what does an anchor do? It keeps the ship on course when wind and waves rage against it. But the anchor of hope is sunk in heaven, not on earth.

Gregory Floyd, A Grief Unveiled

INTRODUCTION

M Y husband, David, and son, Matt, and I were working around the house on a Saturday morning when we heard the sound of helicopters and looked out the window to see black smoke billowing from somewhere in our neighborhood. A house, two cul-de-sacs away, was on fire. David walked over to the house, checked it out, and came back sobered by what he had seen—the house had burned to the ground in a matter of minutes.

When you witness something like that, you can't help but think, *How would I respond if that happened to me? What would I do if I drove up to the house I had left that morning, and it had been destroyed?*

It reminded me of a story I had read that week—a story of loss so astounding that most of us can hardly imagine it. It is the ancient story of a man named Job, a man known, perhaps, as history's most significant sufferer. Job was sitting at home one day when a series of messengers came and told him that all of his livestock and servants had been slaughtered and then that all of his children had perished as the building they were in collapsed. Then, as if losing everything he had and nearly everyone he loved was not enough, Job was stricken with painful sores all over his body.

As I read his story, I was amazed by Job's response to pain and loss. *Would I respond that way to tragedy?* I wondered. I also noticed that Job was specifically chosen to experience great suffering. Evidently he was chosen not because he deserved to suffer or because he was being punished, but because of his great faith. And I wondered about my own faith—if I had the kind of faith that could withstand extreme, undeserved affliction. A faith that would remain when all hope was gone.

But that was before the affliction came. Before the devastating news that changed everything about my life. Before the painful anticipation of death. BEFORE HOPE.

JOB'S JOURNEY

—◇—

THERE was a man named Job who lived in the land of Uz. He was blameless, a man of complete integrity. He feared God and stayed away from evil. He had seven sons and three daughters. He owned seven thousand sheep, three thousand camels, five hundred teams of oxen, and five hundred female donkeys, and he employed many servants. He was, in fact, the richest person in that entire area.

Every year when Job's sons had birthdays, they invited their brothers and sisters to join them for a celebration. On these occasions they would get together to eat and drink. When these celebrations ended—and sometimes they lasted several days—Job would purify his children. He would get up early in the morning and offer a burnt offering for each of them. For Job said to himself, "Perhaps my children have sinned and have cursed God in their hearts." This was Job's regular practice.

One day the angels came to present themselves before the Lord, and Satan the Accuser came with them. "Where have you come from?" the Lord asked Satan.

And Satan answered the Lord, "I have been going back and forth across the earth, watching everything that's going on."

Then the Lord asked Satan, "Have you noticed my servant Job? He is the finest man in all the earth—a man of complete integrity. He fears God and will have nothing to do with evil."

Satan replied to the Lord, "Yes, Job fears God, but not without good reason! You have always protected him and his home and his property from harm. You have made him prosperous in everything he does. Look how rich he is! But take away everything he has, and he will surely curse you to your face!"

"All right, you may test him," the Lord said to Satan. "Do whatever you want with everything he possesses, but don't harm him physically." So Satan left the Lord's presence.

JOB 1:1-12

LOSS

Two weeks after the neighbor's house burned down, I gave birth to a daughter we named Hope. For years we had planned on that name for a daughter, but I never could have dreamed how meaningful it would become.

The doctors were immediately concerned by several "small" problems evident at birth—Hope had club feet, she was very lethargic and unresponsive, she had a flat chin and a large soft spot, she had a tiny indentation on one earlobe, she would not suck, and her hands were turned slightly outward.

On Hope's second day of life, a geneticist who had examined her came to our room. He told us that he suspected Hope had a metabolic disorder called Zellweger Syndrome. Because she was missing something in her cells called peroxisomes, which rid cells of toxins, her systems would slowly shut down.

And then he dropped the bomb that most babies with this syndrome live less than six months. No treatment. No cure. No survivors. I felt like the air had been sucked out of me. While he was talking, I let out a low groan.

To be honest, it just didn't seem real. Sometimes it still doesn't. My husband, David, crawled into the hospital bed with me and we cried and we cried out to God. The next morning when I woke up, I was hoping that perhaps I had dreamed the whole thing—but I hadn't.

We called our pastor and asked him to come see us that morning. I looked at him and said, "Well, I guess here is where the rubber meets the road. Here is where I find out if I really believe what I say I believe." I knew I had to choose how I was going to respond to this incredible disappointment and sorrow.

In the days following the diagnosis, we learned how to feed Hope with a tube and awaited the anticipated onset of seizures. As we began to accept the reality that she would be with us for only a short time, I returned to the story of Job. I wanted to look more closely at how Job responded as his world fell apart.

Perhaps you've experienced your world falling apart. Maybe your marriage has ended, or your parents' marriage has ended. Maybe financial disaster has come your way and you're trying to dig your way out. Maybe your child has rejected your values and rejected you. Maybe you've received the diagnosis you didn't want. Or maybe, like me, you have faced the sorrow and loneliness of losing someone you love.

Do you feel as if your world has fallen apart? If so, you know what it is like to feel hurt and helpless and hopeless in the midst of loss. And perhaps you, too, are wondering if you will ever find your way out of this place of pain.

Throughout the pages of this short book, we're going to look carefully at Job's experience, because Job shows us how a person of faith responds when his world falls apart. We know Job was a great man of faith because the writer tells us so in the first verse of the first chapter, describing Job as a man of complete integrity who feared God and stayed away from evil. And, later in the same chapter, God himself uses these same words to describe Job.

This introduction shows us that Job was devoted to God. He had impeccable character. We could even describe Job as God's friend. In fact, when God endeavored to choose one person he knew would be faithful to him no matter what, he chose Job—with complete confidence. Job must have proved himself faithful over and over for God to have had that kind of confidence in him!

But Satan was skeptical. Satan thought Job was faithful only because Job was supernaturally protected by God and had such a comfortable life, and that if his comfortable life were taken away, Job would turn on God.

At that point, God gave Satan permission to hurt Job. We don't want to hear that, because it just doesn't square with our understanding of a loving God. But it is clear. God gave the permission and set the parameters for Job's suffering.[1]

"'All right, you may test him,' the Lord said to Satan. 'Do whatever you want with everything he possesses, but don't harm him physically'" (Job 1:12).

Do you wonder why God would give permission for Satan to harm Job? More importantly, do you wonder why God has given Satan permission to bring so much pain into *your* life?

Before we try to answer the question "Why?" let's look closely at how Job responded as everything he had and everyone he loved were abruptly ripped away.

We'll see that Job's story is about much more than his suffering. Somehow, along the way, he discovered God in a way he had never known him before. And when his story comes to a close, we see that "the Lord blessed Job in the second half of his life even more than in the beginning. . . . He died, an old man who had lived a long, good life" (Job 42:12, 17).

Isn't that what you and I want, even now, in the midst of our painful circumstances—to understand God like we never have before, to see him as we've never seen him before, to emerge from our days of suffering with God's blessing and with a life that can be described as good?

How did Job move from profound pain to profound blessing? Let's follow Job's steps closely to discover his secret. Let's examine each stepping stone along the way. Let's follow him on the pathway of suffering so that he might lead us to the very heart of God.

One day when Job's sons and daughters were dining at the oldest brother's house, a messenger arrived at Job's home with this news: "Your oxen were plowing, with the donkeys feeding beside them, when the Sabeans raided us. They stole all the animals and killed all the farmhands. I am the only one who escaped to tell you."

While he was still speaking, another messenger arrived with this news: "The fire of God has fallen from heaven and burned up your sheep and all the shepherds. I am the only one who escaped to tell you."

While he was still speaking, a third messenger arrived with this news: "Three bands of Chaldean raiders have stolen your camels and killed your servants. I am the only one who escaped to tell you."

While he was still speaking, another messenger arrived with this news: "Your sons and daughters were feasting in their oldest brother's home. Suddenly, a powerful wind swept in from the desert and hit the house on all sides. The house collapsed, and all your children are dead. I am the only one who escaped to tell you."

Job stood up and tore his robe in grief.

JOB 1:13-20

TEARS

Shortly after Hope died, I was at the cosmetics counter buying some mascara. "Will this mascara run down my face when I cry?" I asked.

The girl behind the counter assured me it wouldn't and asked with a laugh in her voice, "Are you going to be crying?"

"Yes," I answered. "I am."

We had Hope for 199 days. We loved her. We enjoyed her richly and shared her with everyone we could. We held her during her seizures. Then, we let her go.

The day after we buried Hope, my husband said to me, "You know, I think we expected our faith to make this hurt less, but it doesn't. Our faith gave us an incredible amount of strength and encouragement while we had Hope, and we are comforted by the knowledge that she is in heaven. Our faith keeps us from being swallowed by despair. But I don't think it makes our loss hurt any less."

It is only natural that people around me often ask searchingly, "How are you?" And for much of the first year after Hope's death, my answer was, "I'm deeply and profoundly sad." I've been blessed with many people who have been willing to share my sorrow, to just be sad with me. Others, however, seem to want to rush me through my sadness. They want to fix me. But I lost someone I loved dearly, and I'm sad.

Ours is not a culture that is comfortable with sadness. Sadness is awkward. It is unsettling. It ebbs and flows and takes its own shape. It beckons to be shared. It comes out in tears, and we don't quite know what to do with those.

So many people are afraid to bring up my loss. They don't want to upset me. But my tears are the only way I have to release the deep sorrow I feel. I tell people, "Don't worry about crying in front of me, and don't be afraid that you will make me cry! Your tears tell me you care, and my tears tell you that you've touched me in a place that is meaningful to me—and I will never forget your willingness to share my grief."

In fact, those who shed their tears with me show me we are not alone. It often feels like we are carrying this enormous load of sorrow, and when others shed their tears with me, it is as if they are taking a bucketful of sadness and carrying it for me. It is, perhaps, the most meaningful thing anyone can do for me.

Our culture wants to put the Band-Aid of heaven

on the hurt of losing someone we love. Sometimes it seems like the people around us think that because we know the one we love is in heaven, we shouldn't be sad. But they don't understand how far away heaven feels, and how long the future seems as we see before us the years we have to spend on this earth before we see the one we love again.

Fortunately, we are not alone in our sadness. In Isaiah 53:3, the Bible describes God's Son as "a Man of sorrows and acquainted with grief" (NKJV). And so it is in our sadness that we discover a new aspect of God's character and reach a new understanding of him that we could not have known without loss. He is acquainted with grief. He understands. He's not trying to rush us through our sadness. He's sad with us.

The day after we buried Hope, I understood for the first time why so many people choose to medicate their pain in so many harmful ways. That day I tried to sleep it away. And in the days that followed, I discovered that I could not sleep it away, shop it away, eat it away, drink it away, or travel it away.

I just had to feel it. And it hurt. Physically.

I realized I had a choice—I could try to stuff the hurt away in a closet, pretend it wasn't there, and wish it would disappear, or I could bring it out into the open, expose it to the Light, probe it, accept it, and allow it to heal. I chose to face it head-on, trudge through it, feel its full weight, and do my best to confront my feelings of loss and hopelessness with the truth of God's Word at every turn. Even now I can't say I'm healed. Part of my heart is no longer mine. I gave it to Hope and she took it with her, and I will forever feel that amputation.[2] But embracing my grief means allowing it to do its work in me.

That's what Job did. Out of the deepest kind of agony and pain from loss, Job openly mourned. He didn't cover up his sadness or put on a happy face or offer religious-sounding clichés. He tore his robe and shaved his head. He hurt. And he was not ashamed to show how deeply he hurt.

Do you know what it is like to groan with sorrow? Part of being human is that when you lose something or someone that is valuable to you, you agonize over that loss, and there is nothing wrong with that. Your tears do not reflect a lack of faith.

Rather than running from or trying to ignore your grief, would you lean into it? Would you allow it to accomplish its healing work in your heart?

Would you be willing to invite God to walk with you during this sorrowful time so that you might experience his healing presence?

Would you confront your feelings of hopelessness and heartache with truths from God's Word so that it can become a healing power in your heart and mind?

JOB stood up and tore his robe in grief. Then he shaved his head and fell to the ground before God.

JOB 1:20

WORSHIP

I hate to admit it, but for some reason, church has often been one of the hardest places to be since Hope's death. I suppose part of it is the people. Even though they are so kind and caring, there is something inexplicably difficult about a crowd when you are grieving, isn't there? At times I've headed into the building with completely conflicting feelings. Part of me can't stand the idea that perhaps no one will say anything about Hope, while another part of me dreads that so many people will say something to me about her.

But it is not just the people I will encounter that makes going to church so difficult. It's God himself. It's the words we sing during the service that get choked in my throat:

> *Whatever my lot, Thou hast taught me to say,*
> *"It is well, it is well with my soul." . . .*
>
> *Great is Thy faithfulness, Lord, unto me. . . .*

I sing for joy at the work of your hands,
Forever I'll love you, forever I'll stand . . .

It is one thing to go to church; it is another thing to worship. To be honest, sometimes I just don't feel like it. Sometimes I just don't feel like praising and adoring God for who he is and what he has done, which is the essence of worship. To offer up thanksgiving and praise to him sometimes feels dishonest or insincere.

That's why I am so amazed when I consider the story of Job. There was more to Job's initial response to his loss than just mourning and agony. As Job responded to calamity in his life, he fell to the ground before God in worship.

Do you find that an odd response? He'd just lost everything, and yet he fell to the ground to worship God. When I read that I wonder, *How could he have done that?*

Only a person who understood the greatness of God could have worshiped at such a time. This was, perhaps, the first of many times over the coming months and years that Job chose to do what was right rather than to focus completely on his feelings.

Even though Job felt crushed, perhaps even betrayed, he did what he knew was right—he worshiped almighty God.

Job obviously knew how to worship. He didn't have to go to a temple. His faith was so genuine and permeated his life so completely that he recognized he could worship God right where he was, just as he was. For Job, worship was a way of life.

When our skin is pricked by a thorn, what comes out is what's inside: blood. When our lives are pricked by difficulty, what comes out is what's inside. For some of us, it is selfishness, pride, bitterness, and anger that come seeping out. For others, it is the fruit of the Spirit—love, joy, peace, patience, kindness, goodness, faithfulness, gentleness, and self-control (Galatians 5:22-23). What came out when Job was not just pricked, but pierced, was worship.

Often, worship is a matter of obedience. At least it is for me. But, as in many other areas, when I make the choice to be obedient, God changes my feelings, and I come to the place of passionate worship.

You see, we worship because God is worthy, not necessarily because we "feel" like it. In the midst of a crisis, if we only do what we feel like doing, we could remain stuck in a cycle of self-pity. But when we worship, we get our eyes off of ourselves and our sorrow or problems. We focus them on God, and this puts our difficulties into proper perspective.

Most of us think of worship as a Sunday-morning activity in which we gather in a church, sing some songs, and listen to a preacher. Genuine worship, though, is when the words that flow out of our lips and the works that flow out of our lives glorify God and honor him for who he is and what he has done.

We worship when we reflect his glory—his character and likeness—to others in the way we live. And doesn't it seem that everyone around us is watching especially closely when tragedy strikes in our lives?

Surely our worship in the midst of pain and sorrow is particularly precious to God—because it costs us so much. Worship is not made easier, but it becomes all the more meaningful when offered from a heart that is hurting.

The truth is, worship during these times can be some of the most meaningful worship we ever experience. Perhaps we are more fully equipped to worship than ever before because we are acutely aware of our desperate need for God and our own incapacitating weakness. We have our helplessness and inadequacy in proper perspective to God's power and sufficiency.

Do you want to find the heart of God in the darkness of your suffering? In the brokenness of overwhelming grief, would you set aside your feelings of disappointment and confusion—and even anger—and begin to worship God?

When you can't find your own words, would you open to the Psalms and use the words of David in praise and confession and lament?

Would you determine to worship God's worthiness and trust in his faithfulness even when the confusion and disappointment do not immediately disappear?

Worship

Come, Thou Fount of ev'ry blessing,
Tune my heart to sing Thy grace;
Streams of mercy never ceasing,
Call for songs of loudest praise:
Teach me some melodious sonnet,
Sung by flaming tongues above;
Praise His name—I'm fixed upon it—
Name of God's redeeming love.

Hitherto Thy love has blest me;
Thou has bro't me to this place;
And I know Thy hand will bring me
Safely home by Thy good grace.
Jesus sought me when a stranger,
Wand'ring from the fold of God;
He, to rescue me from danger,
Bo't me with His precious blood.

O, to grace how great a debtor
Daily I'm constrained to be!
Let Thy goodness, like a fetter,
Bind my wand'ring heart to Thee.
Prone to wander, Lord, I feel it;
Prone to leave the God I love;
Here's my heart, O, take and seal it;
Seal it for Thy courts above.

ROBERT ROBINSON
adapted by Margaret Clarkson

HE said, "I came naked from my mother's womb, and I will be stripped of everything when I die. The Lord gave me everything I had, and the Lord has taken it away. Praise the name of the Lord!"

JOB 1:21

GRATITUDE

David stayed home with Hope on Wednesdays so I could go to Bible study. One morning in January, I got in the car after class and called him from my mobile phone. He didn't answer, which I thought was strange. So I tried his mobile. He answered.

"Where are you?" I asked.

"We're all fine," he said.

(Now, you know when someone starts with that, we're *not* all fine, right?)

"We're at Dr. Ladd's office, but not for Hope," he continued. "Matt fell in PE this morning and broke off his front tooth."

I took a deep breath and just couldn't say anything for a minute. I guess it hit me in the area of my greatest fear—that Hope wouldn't be our only loss.

That night, as David and I talked about the day, we realized that we both had an unspoken agreement with God that went something like this: "Fine. We will accept losing Hope and all that this brings. But we don't lose Matt. We don't lose each other. No car accidents. No cancer. No financial collapse. This is it!"

But as we voiced our deepest feelings and fears out loud, we realized that we had to let go of those things too. We needed to trust God with everything we had, to open ourselves and say, *God, it is all yours to do with as you will!*

Some days I wonder if the letting go is ever going to stop. Since Hope's death, I have had to let go of her physical body, my dreams for her, and many of her things. I have had to let go of her room and turn it back into a guest room. I have a sweet friend who put together a beautiful scrapbook of Hope's life. Another friend who saw the scrapbook said to me, "I know what you would grab first in a fire!" Then I noticed the pages have already started to become dog-eared and discolored. I feel so protective of the book, but I've realized that I have to be willing to let go of that book, too. To some that may seem a silly sacrifice, but the book represents all my memories of Hope. I have to hold on to those loosely as well.

You see, Hope was a gift. And the appropriate response to a gift is gratitude.

That's what we see in Job. As he fell to the ground to worship God, even though he had just lost everything, Job was thanking God for everything God had given him. When Job said, "The Lord gave me everything I had, and the Lord has taken it away," we see that Job recognized that everything he had was a gift from God and that Job had learned how to hold on to those gifts loosely. Evidently Job, long before, had figured out that his extreme wealth and blessing not only *came* from God but also were *still* God's, while Job himself was just a steward.

How about you? I know you can barely stand to think about being grateful in the midst of your loss. You probably think I'm crazy to even suggest that you could be grateful as you face the empty chair, the empty bank account, the emptiness.

God gives, and God takes away. But let's be honest: We just want him to give, don't we? And we certainly don't want him to take away the things or the people we love.

We tend to think the money in our bank accounts and the possessions we have are ours—that we've earned them. That we deserve them. But the truth is, everything we have is a gift.

There's an old book called *Tracks of a Fellow Struggler*[3] written by John Claypool, who lost a daughter to leukemia. He tells a story of growing up during World War II. When one of his father's business associates went off to war, the man's family went to live elsewhere, and they left behind their washing machine for the Claypool family to use.

Two years passed. The war was over, the friends returned, and they wanted their washing machine back. When they came and took it, young Claypool openly expressed his resentment. His family had grown accustomed to having the washing machine, and it seemed so unfair to have to give it back. His mother wisely pointed out that the washing machine was never theirs in the first place. It was a gift for as long as they were able to use it, and the proper response to a gift is gratitude.

When you come to the place where you recognize that everything you have and everyone you love is a gift, it becomes possible to enjoy those gifts—not with an attitude of greed but with one of gratitude. You and I, like Job, know that God gives and God takes away. And when he takes away, if we're able to focus on the joy of what was given, if only for a time, we take another step down the pathway toward the heart of God.

Would you be willing to thank God for a gift he gave you and has now taken away? Maybe it was your spouse, your reputation, your financial security, your health, your home. . . . *Thank you.*

Would you ask God to help you to loosen your grip on the gifts he has given you so you can feel the freedom of entrusting everything to his care?

Would you welcome God to have his way with your possessions, your position, the people you love? Would you accept his promise that *he can be enough?*

> *Always be joyful. Keep on praying. No matter what happens, always be thankful, for this is God's will for you who belong to Christ Jesus.*
> 1 THESSALONIANS 5:16-18

In *all of this, Job did not sin by blaming God.*

JOB 1:22

BLAME

I'm stunned at how quickly the words "sue him" can come out of my ten-year-old's mouth. A product of our culture, whenever something doesn't seem fair or something bad happens, he is ready to place the blame and to make someone pay.

Oftentimes when unfair, undeserved suffering comes into our lives, we demand to hold someone responsible—the doctor who made a drastic error in judgment, the driver who had too much to drink, the divorce lawyer who drove such a hard bargain.

But the someone we most often hold responsible for the suffering in our lives is God.

Is that where you find yourself today? Are you blaming God for something that has happened in your life? Have you been carrying it around for a long time now?

Blaming God. We might not say we blame God outright, but we become bitter—bitter toward the alcoholic father or violent attacker, not seeing that

bitterness is ultimately blaming God for the circumstances of our lives.

When trouble comes, we think, "I don't deserve
this!" But wait. What would your life be like if you *did*
get what you really deserve? Were it not for the grace
of God, for his mercy, what would your life be like?
Think about that for a minute.

Evidently Job did not have the mind-set that he
"deserved" his comfortable, blessed life. Amazingly,
we see that Job did not blame God for taking away
everything and everyone he loved so dearly. Somehow, Job avoided blaming God for his devastating
circumstances.

So how did Job do it? And more importantly, how
can you and I, when we've lost so much, avoid becoming bitter, blaming people? First, I think we need
a clear understanding of where the blame belongs.

Much of the evil that happens in this world, in
your world, in my world, is the natural consequence
of humanity's sinfulness. Don't blame God—blame
sin. Blame Adam. The book of Romans helps us
understand:

> *When Adam sinned, sin entered the entire
> human race. Adam's sin brought death, so death
> spread to everyone, for everyone sinned.*
>
> ROMANS 5:12

> *Against its will, everything on earth was sub-
> jected to God's curse. All creation anticipates the*

> *day when it will join God's children in glorious*
> *freedom from death and decay.*
>
> ROMANS 8:20-21

Death, disease, destruction—these are all the result of living in a world where sin has taken root and corrupted everything. It is this curse of sin that required Jesus to become flesh and to die. He died to overcome the curse of sin—not only in our individual lives but in all of creation. In fact, because of his sufficient sacrifice, the day is coming when we will be set free from this curse.

> *Then I saw a new heaven and a new earth, for*
> *the old heaven and the old earth had disap-*
> *peared. . . . I heard a loud shout from the throne,*
> *saying, "Look, the home of God is now among his*
> *people! He will live with them, and they will be*
> *his people. God himself will be with them. He will*
> *remove all of their sorrows, and there will be no*
> *more death or sorrow or crying or pain. For the*
> *old world and its evils are gone forever." . . . No*
> *longer will anything be cursed. For the throne of*
> *God and of the Lamb will be there, and his*
> *servants will worship him.*
>
> REVELATION 21:1, 3-4; 22:3

For now, we still live in a world that is under a curse. And, unless we follow Job's example, it's easy to blame God. I think the key to Job's ability to keep from blaming God is in the first line of his story, which says that Job "feared God."

What does it mean to "fear" God?[4] It certainly goes beyond simply being afraid of God. It is a profound sense of reverential awe toward God. But really it is even more than that. The fear of God is better described than defined. It is displayed in a person's character and conduct. A person who fears God recognizes God's authority over every area of his life. He has a desire to obey God's clear commands in Scripture. He recognizes his complete dependence upon God for everything he has and everything he is. He approaches every aspect of life with an aim to glorify God. And when life deals him a blow, his fear of God is revealed more completely.

In Exodus 20:20, we read of Moses telling God's people, "Don't be afraid . . . for God has come in this way to show you his awesome power. From now on, let your fear of him keep you from sinning!" Moses makes it clear that there is a difference between being afraid of God and fearing God. Simply being afraid of God leads to distrust and disobedience, but the fear of God keeps us from a life marked by sin.

In the seeming unfairness of losing someone or something we love, fellow believers sometimes encourage us to express our anger toward God freely. And certainly God can handle our honest emotions. But the fear of God holds our tongue when we want to accuse God of wrongdoing; it halts our defiant finger-wagging; it humbles us in the midst of our self-righteous anger.

If you desire to come out on the other side of your suffering without the baggage of blaming God and all of the bitterness and brokenness that blaming brings, then you must understand and grow in the fear of God. The Bible says that the fear of God is the beginning of wisdom (Proverbs 9:10). Do you really want to come to a better understanding of the big picture? The starting place is to develop a healthy fear of God.

If you want to fear God, you need to know him. Knowing him requires a consistent, comprehensive study of God's Word. As we regularly encounter God in his Word, and as the Holy Spirit works it into our lives, we see God's majesty and power, his holiness and wisdom, and his love expressed in his grace and mercy to us. We come to admire his attributes and stand amazed at his love. And, even when undeserved suffering threatens to crush us, we're able to avoid the sin of cursing and blaming God.

Would you begin today to grow in the fear of God by a careful and consistent study of what he says about himself in the Bible?

Would you be honest with God about your feelings and questions, without a spirit of resistance and rebellion?

Would you place the blame for your suffering where it belongs—on sinful humanity—rather than cursing and blaming God?

THEN the Lord asked Satan, "Have you noticed my servant Job? He . . . has maintained his integrity, even though you persuaded me to harm him without cause."

Satan replied to the Lord, "Skin for skin—he blesses you only because you bless him. A man will give up everything he has to save his life. But take away his health, and he will surely curse you to your face!"

"All right, do with him as you please," the Lord said to Satan. "But spare his life." So Satan left the Lord's presence, and he struck Job with a terrible case of boils from head to foot.

Then Job scraped his skin with a piece of broken pottery as he sat among the ashes. His wife said to him, "Are you still trying to maintain your integrity? Curse God and die."

But Job replied, "You talk like a godless woman. Should we accept only good things from the hand of God and never anything bad?"

JOB 2:3-10

SUFFERING

I can remember where I was on the road near our house when I prayed, "God, bring affliction into my life, if that's what it takes to know you more intimately." I had the sense that God was preparing me for something, but I didn't know what it was. If I had, I don't think I would have prayed that prayer.

I had noticed that very few people go through life without some sort of intense suffering. I guess I also had the sense that it was my turn. I had not known a great deal of sorrow in my life. And while I would not describe my life as easy, I've certainly been incredibly blessed. So as I looked at the world around me, I wondered, *When will it be my turn for pain?*

You probably did not invite difficulty into your life. More likely, it was thrust upon you. In fact, most of us spend our lives doing everything we can to *avoid* suffering. In today's modern world, we expect a cure for every illness, a replacement for every loss, a fix for every failure. We are shocked and shaken when hardship comes our way.

But look around. How many people do you know who have escaped experiencing profound difficulty at some point in their lives? Look at the Scriptures. Can you find a person in the Bible—even the godliest of persons—who did not suffer greatly?

Job wasn't looking for suffering, and yet it didn't seem to catch him off guard. Just when his wife wanted him to completely give up on life and give up on God because of his suffering, Job said to her, "Should we accept only good things from the hand of God and never anything bad?"

Job's acceptance and even expectation of both good and bad things from God is in sharp contrast to our expectations today, which is why we have such a hard time responding to suffering in a godly way like Job did. We have an unspoken expectation that a *good God* will bring only what we consider to be *good things* into our lives. We never expect him to *allow* and perhaps even *bring* difficulty into our lives. But he does.

Does that surprise you? Does that bother you?

We might not say it, but in the back of our minds we somehow think that because Job was so godly, he should have been spared from pain. But the truth is, often people who follow God suffer—not less but more. Have you ever noticed that people who suffer are marked with a beauty, a deepening, a transformation?[5] This only occurs, however, when they enter the suffering and look around for God in the midst of it.

Otherwise, they are marked with bitterness and emptiness.

"But," you say, "God does not willingly afflict his children." That's true.

> *For men are not cast off by the Lord forever.*
> *Though he brings grief, he will show compassion,*
> *so great is his unfailing love. For he does not*
> *willingly bring affliction or grief to the chil-*
> *dren of men.*
>
> LAMENTATIONS 3:31-33 (NIV)

What does this mean? No suffering for God's children? No.

It means no *meaningless* suffering. If God has allowed suffering into your life, it is for a purpose. A good purpose. A holy purpose.

The world tells us to run from suffering, to avoid it at all costs, to cry out to heaven to take it away. Few of us would *choose* to suffer. Yet when we know that God has allowed suffering into our lives for a purpose, we can embrace it instead of running from it, and we can seek God in the midst of suffering. Accepting suffering drives us deeper in our devotion.

> *Anyone who intends to come with me has to let*
> *me lead. You're not in the driver's seat—I am.*
> *Don't run from suffering; embrace it. Follow*
> *me and I'll show you how. Self-help is no help at*
> *all. Self-sacrifice is the way, my way, to finding*

*yourself, your true self. What good would it do
to get everything you want and lose you, the
real you?*

LUKE 9:23-25 *(THE MESSAGE)*

Jesus is suggesting that we do more than simply
endure suffering. He's inviting us to stop feeling sorry
for ourselves and focus instead on learning from suffering. Not only does Jesus invite us to embrace suffering, but he also shows us what that looks like.
According to Hebrews 5:7-9, "During the days of
Jesus' life on earth, he offered up prayers and peti-
tions with loud cries and tears to the one who could
save him from death, and he was heard because of his
reverent submission. Although he was a son, he
learned obedience from what he suffered and, once
made perfect, he became the source of eternal salvation for all who obey him" (NIV).

I have clung to this verse in the lowest days of my
grief. In it I see that sometimes God's plan includes
suffering and death. Amazingly, his plan to redeem
the world and to make a way for you and me to spend
eternity with him included the suffering and death of
his own Son. It helps me to know that Jesus wrestled
with that plan even as he submitted to it.

Have you cried out to God in frustration, with
questions about how he could have the power to heal
and yet choose *not* to heal the one you love? Have you
agonized in an effort to reconcile your understanding

of a loving God with One who allowed the accident, the atrocity, the abuse? I have. And we're not alone.

When you groan because there are no words for the hurt, when you cry out to God with hot tears, when you agonize over his plan that has caused you such pain, look at Hebrews 5:7-9 and see that Jesus understands! He understands what it is like to cry out to the Father, who has the power to make another way, enact another plan . . . but chooses not to.

In fact, the prophet Isaiah wrote, "Yet it pleased the Lord to bruise Him; He has put Him to grief" (Isaiah 53:10, NKJV). It *pleased* the Father? How can that be?

The answer is that God was pleased by what Jesus' death accomplished for you and for me. He was pleased to demonstrate his love for the human race through such a significant sacrifice.

Amazingly, history's most evil act brought about the greatest good of all time. Though those who put Jesus on the cross meant to do evil against him, God used it for good, in order to bring many to himself.

The Cross, then, is the ultimate example of God's ability to work all things together for good—even the most wicked deed Darkness ever conceived.

Surely if God would require such intense suffering of his own Son, whom he loved, to accomplish a holy purpose, he has a purpose for your pain and for my pain. And perhaps part of that purpose is to learn obedience from what we suffer.

Why has God allowed so much suffering in your life? Ultimately, the purpose is not to disfigure you for life but to mold you into a person who thinks and acts and looks like Christ.[6]

Every difficulty—from the minor irritation of a broken piece of crystal to the piercing pain of a broken relationship—God has allowed every one for the singular and supreme purpose of transforming your character into the likeness of his Son.

Sometimes it requires pain to refine our character and to remove our selfish, sinful attitudes. Pain can do that. Or, pain can make us bitter. We can just become bitter when we don't get what we want out of life.

When I was in junior high, I read a couple of books by an author named Bob Benson. Since living in Nashville, I've had the privilege of becoming friends with his widow, Peggy. Peggy came over when Hope was a few weeks old, and I told her I'd been thinking a lot about a story Bob relates in *He Speaks Softly*.[7] He tells of how, whenever he was speaking at a retreat, he would ask the people there to take out a piece of paper and fold it in half. He would instruct them to make a list on the top part of the paper of everything bad that had ever happened to them. Then he would tell them to make a list on the bottom part of the paper of the best things that had ever happened to them.

What people found was that there were many things from the top of the page that they also wanted to include in the list at the bottom of the page. Experiences they had labeled as the worst things that had ever happened to them had, over time, become some of the best things that had ever happened to them. That's because God uses the painful, difficult experiences of life for our ultimate good! In many cases they become the best things that ever happened to us.

Early on in my journey, I said to God, "Okay, if I have to go through this, then give me everything. Teach me everything you want to teach me through this. Don't let this incredible pain be wasted in my life!" I know God has a purpose for allowing this pain into my life and that it is for my ultimate good. So I can actually embrace my pain. Would you believe I can thank God for this bitter but rich experience? I can, because I know God is good—that he allows good and bad into our lives and that we can trust him with both.

And I believe God has a purpose for the pain in your life that is for your ultimate good, even though everything about it looks and feels bad.

Rather than running from your suffering or trying to pray it away, would you embrace it and look for God in it?

Would you allow suffering to be your teacher so that you can learn something from it you never could have learned from comfort and ease?

Would you hold tight to the truth that there is no meaningless suffering for a child of God, and would you refuse to allow pain to be wasted in your life?

Dear brothers and sisters, whenever trouble comes your way, let it be an opportunity for joy. For when your faith is tested, your endurance has a chance to grow. So let it grow, for when your endurance is fully developed, you will be strong in character and ready for anything.

JAMES 1:2-4

AT last Job spoke, and he cursed the day of his birth. He said: "Cursed be the day of my birth, and cursed be the night when I was conceived. Let that day be turned to darkness. Let it be lost even to God on high, and let it be shrouded in darkness. Yes, let the darkness and utter gloom claim it for its own. Let a black cloud overshadow it, and let the darkness terrify it. Let that night be blotted off the calendar, never again to be counted among the days of the year, never again to appear among the months. Let that night be barren. Let it have no joy.

"Why didn't I die at birth as I came from the womb? Why did my mother let me live? Why did she nurse me at her breasts? For if I had died at birth, I would be at peace now, asleep and at rest.

"I cannot eat for sighing; my groans pour out like water. What I always feared has happened to me. What I dreaded has come to be. I have no peace, no quietness. I have no rest; instead, only trouble comes."

JOB 3:1-7, 11-13, 24-26

DESPAIR

Sorrow upon sorrow. Difficulty and more difficulty. Does that describe your life? Why is it that in the middle of a crisis, the car breaks down and the refrigerator stops working? Doesn't it seem like we should get a pass on the minor irritations of life when we are in the midst of a tragedy?

For many of us it is not just one painful experience or circumstance but troubles that seem to multiply. It can seem like a conspiracy meant to destroy us. And we feel beaten down, discouraged. We wonder if the sun is ever going to come out again. And despair sets in.

After Hope was born, my husband and I made a difficult decision. We knew that because we both carry the recessive gene trait for Zellweger Syndrome, any child of ours would have a 25 percent chance of being born with the fatal syndrome. Even though we thought we might be willing to take the chance, we felt we could not risk putting our son, Matt, and our parents through such a sorrowful experience again. So we took surgical steps to prevent a future pregnancy.

Evidently that procedure reversed itself, and today as I write, I find myself pregnant.

Upon making the startling discovery, we felt a mixture of emotions. We felt afraid as we considered what might be ahead in having and then losing another child. We felt a cautious joy as we considered that we might have another healthy child to raise and enjoy.

But after a series of prenatal tests, we now know that we will indeed be welcoming another child with Zellweger Syndrome into our family—this time, a boy, who will also have a very short and difficult life.

It is much different this time, since with Hope, we didn't know until she was born that she suffered from the syndrome. We didn't know what her life or her death would be like. This time, we know. So as we anticipate the arrival of this child, we anticipate both the joy of loving him and the pain of losing him.

Some days, I wonder how we will ever absorb another loss. I still feel battered from the last storm, and another one is headed our direction. In many ways, it doesn't seem fair.

I wonder if that is how Job felt. There he was, in the throes of grief over losing all of his property and all of his family. And then came the sores. From the soles of his feet to the top of his head—itchy, oozing, infected sores.

I imagine Job crying out, "All this, and now boils all over my body too?!"

Perhaps those boils were the final straw, the final unfairness that plunged him into a deep desperation. He "cursed the day of his birth." Hmmm. That doesn't seem very godly. But this godly man, Job, was honest, and he admitted to his discouragement and despair.

Frankly, I love it that we see the real Job here, don't you? To this point, he has seemed a little too perfect, but we see now that he was hurt. He was angry. He was disappointed. And he was honest about it with God. His complaining to God was bitter. What I love here is to see that God, in return, appreciated Job's honesty. In fact, when we get to the end of the book of Job, we discover that God commended Job specifically for his honesty—his honesty about his feelings as well as his honesty about God—while God condemned the self-righteous rantings of Job's friends.

Job was so discouraged he wanted to die.

> *Oh, that I might have my request, that God would grant my hope. I wish he would crush me. I wish he would reach out his hand and kill me.*
>
> JOB 6:8-9

Then he adds these interesting words:

At least I can take comfort in this: Despite the pain, I have not denied the words of the Holy One.

JOB 6:10

Job wouldn't take his own life, but he wanted God to take it and God wouldn't. Yet even in this place of un-speakable pain, Job found consolation in the fact that he had not denied God's Word. He had not turned his back on God.

Sometimes it feels like there is absolutely nothing to ease the pain, doesn't it? People ask what they can do for us, but we know there is nothing they can do to make the hurting go away. In our discouragement, we can be tempted to give up on God and stop pray-ing, wondering, *What good is it anyway?*

Sometimes what God has allowed into our lives is so bitter that we're hurt and angry and don't even want to talk to him about it.

But where does that leave us?

On our own. No resources, no truth to dispel the despair, no hope.

The truth is, there is no comfort to be found away from God; at least, there is no lasting, deep, satisfying comfort. Revenge, ritual, retreat—they don't bring any lasting relief from the pain. Only the truth of God's Word, the tenderness of his welcome, the touch of his healing presence bring the kind of com-fort we crave. Only his promises of purpose in this life and perfection in the life to come offer us any kind of real hope to hold on to.

Do you find yourself wanting to leave the faith you've claimed now that it has been put to the test of adversity? So where will you go? In your discouragement, where will you find the comfort you so desperately crave?

We can find the same consolation Job found in the midst of utter despair. Despite our feelings of discouragement we can hold on to God's promises, hold on to what we know about who he is and how he works. Even though we don't understand, and it is so dark we cannot see to take a step forward, we can choose to hang on, to keep trusting, to keep believing God's Word.

As my husband and I look into the future, that is what we're determined to do. We've been there before, and we know the darkness that is about to sweep over us. This is not the path we would have chosen, but it is the pathway God has set before us. So, here in the dark, we set off on another journey, knowing that each stepping stone along the way will come at great cost. We are guided by a deep desire to please God and by a yearning to discover, along the way, the very heart of God.

In the midst of your despair, would you search for the simple joy of pleasing God and begin to see the clouds lift from your life?

In spite of your questions and confusion about

God's goodness, would you hold firm in believing God's Word, which tells us he is our refuge and strength?

Would you determine to keep talking to God and keep reading his Word in the midst of your despair until he brings you from the darkness into the light?

Even the darkness will not be dark to you.
PSALM 139:12 (NIV)

WHY *won't you leave me alone—even for a moment? Have I*
sinned? What have I done to you, O watcher of all humanity?
Why have you made me your target?

JOB 7:19-20

WHY?

Why? Why me? Why this? Why now? Are there any more persistent questions on your mind? From the depths of your soul, don't you hunger to see the bigger picture, to see a purpose for your pain? My husband and I do. Today we wonder, *Why again?*

You and I want to understand why we are suffering. And Job asked the same question. Job struggled and questioned God in a quest to understand the answer to that big question we all have when something bad happens: *Why?*

When we read Job's story, we see that his friends had all kinds of answers for him, although none of these answers rang true to Job. It wasn't that Job had stopped searching for answers. He just knew that listening to his friends would not get his questions answered. He needed to hear from God himself, so he openly questioned God. What is amazing to me is that Job could question God so boldly and yet not sin! But that is the case.

It is the same for you and me. God doesn't mind our search for understanding. Believe me, I've been looking for the purposes in my pain. God is showing me some, but I don't know that I'll ever see the complete picture in this life. And I don't think Job did either.

Job asked God, "Why?" but it was asked in a spirit of submission to God, with full confidence that God was using the pain in his life for a purpose. Job stood firm with complete confidence that God *did* have a purpose, and he waited for God to reveal it to him, at least in part.

> *God might kill me, but I cannot wait. I am*
> *going to argue my case with him. But this is*
> *what will save me: that I am not godless. If*
> *I were, I would be thrown from his presence.*
>
> JOB 13:15-16

Shortly after Hope's birth, we sent out a card to everyone we knew, telling them about Hope's condition and explaining that her life would be very short. We closed by saying, "Our desire is that God would be glorified in our lives and in Hope's life in the months and years to come." From what I know of Scripture, I believe that we have the ability to bring glory to God in how we respond and deal day by day with this difficulty. I believe that the purpose of Hope's short life, and my life, was and is to glorify God.

Why?

For several years, my husband and I have been narrators for the Good Friday service at our church. Each year, we read the same lines, retelling the story of Creation and Redemption.

But the year Hope was alive, the words seemed to leap off the page. No longer was it necessary for me to interpret the whole of Scripture in my efforts to understand God's purpose in Hope's life. That night, I read it clearly in Jesus' own words, spoken in response to the disciples and recorded in John 9, when they asked why the man was born blind.

> *"Rabbi, who sinned, this man or his parents, that he was born blind?"*
> *"Neither this man nor his parents sinned,"*
> *said Jesus, "but this happened so that the work*
> *of God might be displayed in his life."*
>
> JOHN 9:2-3 (NIV)

Are you asking God why he has allowed you to suffer so much? There is the answer: "so that the work of God might be displayed in [your] life." Instead of continuing to ask, "Why?" would you change your question to, "For what purpose?"

The purpose in the blind man's suffering, in Hope's suffering, and in your suffering is the same: to display the glory of God.

How do you display the glory of God? You reflect his character. Instead of demanding an answer, you decide to trust him, recognizing that your circumstances provide an unparalleled opportunity to glorify God just by your trust in his unseen purpose.

Trusting God when the miracle does not come, when the urgent prayer gets no answer, when there is only darkness—this is the kind of faith God values perhaps most of all. This is the kind of faith that can be developed and displayed only in the midst of difficult circumstances.[8] This is the kind of faith that cannot be shaken because it is the result of having been shaken.[9]

Though his world had been shaken, we see that Job was still firm in his faith. Right in the middle of his "why" questions, Job said:

> But as for me, I know that my Redeemer lives,
> and that he will stand upon the earth at last.
> And after my body has decayed, yet in my body
> I will see God! I will see him for myself. Yes,
> I will see him with my own eyes. I am over-
> whelmed at the thought!

JOB 19:25-27

Somehow Job saw into the distant future and he recognized the only hope you and I have in the midst of the pain of this life—our suffering Savior. He saw a Redeemer. He saw God in Jesus Christ, who would take the pieces of Job's broken life and make something beautiful out of them.

Why?

He recognized that the process of understanding, of answering the question "Why?" would not be complete in this lifetime—that only in the life to come, in the presence of God, would it all become clear. And Job kept walking in the darkness.

Would you be willing to stop asking, "Why?" and begin asking, "For what purpose?"

Would you take comfort and find confidence in knowing that although the purpose in your suffering may be unseen, God does have a purpose, and part of that purpose is to display his work in your life?

Would you look beyond this life and embrace the Redeemer, who will take the pieces of your life and transform them into something beautiful if you invite him to do so?

> *That is why we never give up. Though our bodies are dying, our spirits are being renewed every day. For our present troubles are quite small and won't last very long. Yet they produce for us an immeasurably great glory that will last forever! So we don't look at the troubles we can see right now; rather, we look forward to what we have not yet seen. For the troubles we see will soon be over, but the joys to come will last forever.*
>
> 2 CORINTHIANS 4:16-18

"I myself will see him. . . . How my heart yearns within me!"

JOB 19:27 (NIV)

ETERNITY

Do you find yourself thinking much more about heaven these days because someone you love is there, because it seems you may be there soon, or because you long to escape the pain of your life on this earth? Do you find yourself, like Job, *yearning* for heaven?

Before losing Hope, I never really understood why people find such comfort in knowing their loved one is in heaven, but I do now. When you lose someone you love, heaven becomes much more of a reality, much more than a theological concept or theatrical cliché.

In the midst of his suffering, Job's deepest desire was not just for the suffering to end but for eternity in the presence of God to begin.

I have come to the place where I believe a yearning for heaven is one of the purposes and one of the privileges of suffering and of losing someone you love. I never had that yearning before, but I do now. You see, a piece of me is there. And all too soon, I will have *two* children waiting for me there. I now see in a much fuller way that this life is just a shadow of our real life—of eternal life in the presence of God.

Have you ever noticed how many of the older hymns have a "heaven" verse about how great it is going to be in the "sweet by and by"? But we don't really talk about or sing about heaven that much today because we don't really *yearn* for heaven—because we're so comfortable right here.

We tend to think this life on earth is all there is, and we certainly live that way much of the time. God wants to radically alter that perspective. He wants us to live with an eternal perspective, putting life on this earth in its proper place and living in anticipation of an eternity in his presence.

If we really believe that true life, fullness of joy, and freedom from pain is found in an eternity in God's presence, why do we cling to this earthly life with such vigor?

I did not want to lose Hope. I would have liked to watch her grow. I would have liked to have known her as an adult, to have had a grown daughter who looked like me and talked like me to be my friend in my old age. But I also know that this life is filled with pain, and I don't believe it is a tragedy that Hope had the opportunity to be spared from the evil and pain of this life and instead be in the presence of God.

That is what I believe. It is not necessarily how I *feel*. But my belief does make a difference in how I feel.

A Scripture that has shown me God's perspective and has helped me change my own is Isaiah 57:1-2:

> *The righteous pass away; the godly often die*
> *before their time. And no one seems to care or*
> *wonder why. No one seems to understand that*
> *God is protecting them from the evil to come.*
> *For the godly who die will rest in peace.*

There is no tragedy in being ushered quickly from this life to the next when that next life is spent in the presence of God. There is nothing to fear. The only real tragedy is a life that ends without the hope of eternal life in the presence of God. When a person chooses to reject the free gift of eternal life God has offered through a relationship with his Son, *that* is a tragedy.

Do you find yourself yearning for heaven in the midst of your sorrow or difficulty? Perhaps that is part of the purpose in your pain—a new perspective, a proper perspective, about life on this earth and the life after. Jesus said,

> *Don't be troubled. You trust God, now trust in*
> *me. There are many rooms in my Father's home,*
> *and I am going to prepare a place for you. If this*
> *were not so, I would tell you plainly.*

JOHN 14:1-2

I'm counting on it. I believe that one day I will not only see Hope and our son again, I'll see God face-to-face! That makes a difference in how I grieve and in how I live today.

Would you choose to place higher value on eternity than you place on this life?

Would you recognize that often what *feels* like a tragedy is not, in reality and in light of eternity, a tragedy?

Would you allow God to transform your perspective by meditating on his words about eternity?

> *We've been given a glimpse of the real thing, our true home, our resurrection bodies! The Spirit of God whets our appetite by giving us a taste of what's ahead. He puts a little of heaven in our hearts so that we'll never settle for less.*
>
> 2 CORINTHIANS 5:4-5 *(THE MESSAGE)*

THREE of Job's friends were Eliphaz the Temanite, Bildad the Shuhite, and Zophar the Naamathite. When they heard of the tragedy he had suffered, they got together and traveled from their homes to comfort and console him. When they saw Job from a distance, they scarcely recognized him. Wailing loudly, they tore their robes and threw dust into the air over their heads to demonstrate their grief. Then they sat on the ground with him for seven days and nights. And no one said a word, for they saw that his suffering was too great for words.

JOB 2:11-13

COMFORTERS

Early in our journey with Hope, I believed that I'd have to give people a lot of grace, thinking that many people would say the wrong thing. But really I can count on one hand the comments that I could have gone without.

The first came from a woman who started into a long sermon that I don't remember much of except that it included the statement that this was "for the best." To tell you the truth, I wanted to tell her to shut up.

Then there was the girl who talked with David. It seems as if people have a natural tendency to want us to know they can relate to our pain, and usually, that is a good thing. That's what she was trying to do. At that point, we fed Hope with a tube we threaded down her throat so the formula went right into her tummy. The girl said, "This may sound trivial, but recently my cat was really sick and I had to feed her with a tube, so I kind of know what you're going through." It was all my husband could do to keep from saying, "You know what? That *does* sound trivial."

I'm not sure why, but we have this tendency to want to compare pain. This is harder than that . . . this is easier than that. . . . I think I'm figuring out that you really can't compare pain. It all just hurts.

But to tell you the truth, it hasn't been what people have said but what they *haven't* said that has been the most difficult thing to deal with.

Two weeks before Hope died, I was talking to a woman whose child had died from a heart defect at nine months of age. She told me that the hardest thing for her was when people didn't say anything after her son died. She said, "I wanted to tell them, 'How could you add to my pain by ignoring it?'"

My husband discovered exactly how she felt when he went into the office for the first time after Hope's death. He had a meeting with someone from outside the company—someone who should have known, and probably did know, Hope had died. He came into my husband's office talking a mile a minute but said nothing about our loss. It was the first of many times we experienced the pain of words not spoken.

I've tried not to judge too harshly, because I know I've done the same thing. I know there have been times I've avoided people who were hurting, afraid to bring it up or afraid I would say the wrong thing. Mostly, I just wanted to avoid the awkwardness. I hope I never do that again, but I'm sure I've done it more times than I would like to admit.

I can think of many times when I finally got to the store and bought the perfect card which, unsent, slowly became dog-eared on my dresser. As time went by, I didn't send it because I was embarrassed that it had taken so long. I guess I was hoping that the person who was hurting wouldn't notice that he or she hadn't heard from me. But now I've learned that every person's effort to acknowledge my loss—no matter how small, no matter how much time has passed—is significant and remembered.

Most who have been courageous and kind enough to express their sorrow for us have done so beautifully, even if all they could say was, "I don't really know what to say."

Throughout the story of Job, we read that he not only had to deal with his suffering but also with the response of all his friends who, in many ways, *added* to his suffering.

Job's friends pointed fingers, pontificated, probed. But you know what? I think they were doing the best they could. At the beginning we see that they came to him and wept and mourned with him in silence. But then they made their first mistake—they started talking. And they didn't know what they were talking about.

Then Eliphaz the Temanite replied to Job:
"Will you be patient and let me say a word?
For who could keep from speaking out?"

JOB 4:1-2

When we are plunged into difficult situations, part of the difficulty is dealing with those around us, some of whom try to explain God without knowing what they're talking about. (Sound familiar?)

I like the way Eugene Peterson paraphrases Job's response to his outspoken friends. He says, "I've had all I can take of your talk. What a bunch of miserable comforters!" (Job 16:1-2, *THE MESSAGE*).

Far from having a miserable bunch of comforters, I was blessed with many people who not only knew what to say but also showed they cared in all kinds of creative ways. There was Joanna, who worked to get just the right floral arrangement for Hope's casket. Her plan was to make a wreath out of it for me, but in the days following the service I found that watching the flowers dry and decay became a painful picture of what was happening to Hope's body in the grave. So I called her and she came over and got rid of all the fading flowers in the house. Our friend Jan took us on a river cruise on her fancy boat, and we called the day "Hope Floats." Lori let me talk and let me cry. She held me as I cried after I took Hope's car seat out of the car for the last time. Mary Grace set up a schedule for people to come to our home to help with household tasks or simply to sit and rock Hope. Mary Bess organized meals for us throughout Hope's entire life and in the months following her death. Sue taught the Bible study from which I learned so much that carried me through the crisis. My friend Angela listened to me vent the pain of my deepest regrets. Marty came when I called her in the middle of the night because Hope wouldn't stop crying. She came when I called her in the middle of the night to tell her Hope was gone. Marty came when I just didn't have the strength to clean out Hope's room by myself.

These are just a few of the friends who were there for me.

But I wouldn't be truthful if I didn't tell you that I also have friends who disappeared. Friends who were too busy and didn't seem to—or perhaps didn't know how to—care. I have had to ask God to work in me to forgive them and to accept their limitations.

I wonder how Job was able to get past all the accusations his friends sent his way. It must have helped that God expressed his own anger:

After the Lord had finished speaking to Job, he said to Eliphaz the Temanite: "I am angry with you and with your two friends, for you have not been right in what you said about me, as my servant Job was. Now take seven young bulls and seven rams and go to my servant Job and offer a burnt offering for yourselves. My servant

> *Job will pray for you, and I will accept his*
> *prayer on your behalf. I will not treat you as*
> *you deserve, for you have not been right in what*
> *you said about me, as my servant Job was."*
>
> *So Eliphaz the Temanite, Bildad the Shuhite,*
> *and Zophar the Naamathite did as the Lord*
> *commanded them, and the Lord accepted Job's*
> *prayer.*
>
> *When Job prayed for his friends, the Lord*
> *restored his fortunes. In fact, the Lord gave him*
> *twice as much as before!*
>
> JOB 42:7-10

I look at Job's example, and I see that he prayed for his friends and that "the Lord accepted Job's prayer" (Job 42:9).

I find it somewhat curious that God's instructions to Job were to pray for his friends, until I realize how difficult it is for me to be unforgiving toward someone I am praying for. I wonder if that is why God gave Job those instructions.

If you and I want to be free of the bitterness that estranges us from others and eats away at our own struggle to find joy again, we are going to have to forgive and pray for the friends who have let us down. They might not deserve it. In fact, they probably don't. But then, we don't forgive people because they deserve it; we forgive them because we've been forgiven so much by God and because we want to keep in close relationship with God. And the benefit is that through forgiving, we're set free. When we are able to accept what others have to offer in our time of sorrow, as well as their limitations, we are no longer bound by our expectations or embittered by disappointment in others.

Have you been surrounded by a bunch of miserable comforters on your pathway of suffering? Would you be willing to begin to pray for them so that God might free you from the unforgiveness that has you tied in knots?

Would you extend grace to those who say the wrong thing or nothing at all?

Would you learn from the mistakes as well as the example of others so that you will become the kind of comforter who softens the pain of others?

He comforts us in all our troubles so that we can comfort others. When others are troubled, we will be able to give them the same comfort God has given us. You can be sure that the more we suffer for Christ, the more God will shower us with his comfort through Christ. So when we are weighed down with troubles, it is for your benefit and salvation! For when God comforts us, it is so that we, in turn, can be an encouragement to you. Then you can patiently endure the same things we suffer. We are confident that as you share in suffering, you will also share God's comfort.
2 Corinthians 1:4-7

THEN the Lord answered Job from the whirlwind:

"Who is this that questions my wisdom with such ignorant words? Brace yourself, because I have some questions for you, and you must answer them.

"Where were you when I laid the foundations of the earth? Tell me, if you know so much. Do you know how its dimensions were determined and who did the surveying? What supports its foundations, and who laid its cornerstone as the morning stars sang together and all the angels shouted for joy?"

JOB 38:1-7

MYSTERY

Silence. Sometimes what causes us the most pain and confusion is not what God says to us but the fact that in the midst of difficulty he seems to say nothing at all. Has God been silent in your life as you've been waiting for answers?

That's how it was for Job. He wanted to hear from God. He wanted to understand why he was suffering. He wanted God to clear his name. "Let the Almighty answer me," he said (Job 31:35, NIV).

Finally, after all the questioning and struggle, in a voice from out of a storm, God spoke.

God asked where Job was when God began the work of Creation. What had Job done to call the universe into being, to create his own life, or to make possible the existence of his possessions or his children or his health?[10]

You might expect God to have answered all of those chapters of questions from Job and his friends, who had been waxing eloquent about God and how he works. You might think God would have set the record straight on all the fine points. But that isn't what he did. He answered Job's questions with his own set of questions—four chapters of them—basically reminding Job that he was questioning almighty God.

God didn't explain. He didn't reveal his master plan. Instead, he revealed himself, and in the midst of his awesome presence, Job's questions were not answered—they simply disappeared.[11]

> *Then the Lord said to Job, "Do you still want to argue with the Almighty? You are God's critic, but do you have the answers?"*
>
> *Then Job replied to the Lord, "I am nothing— how could I ever find the answers? I will put my hand over my mouth in silence. I have said too much already. I have nothing more to say."*
>
> JOB 40:1-5

In his response, God did not explain suffering or how to avoid suffering. Suffering is a mystery . . . and Job came to respect the mystery.[12] Job came to understand that because he knew *who God is,* he can accept *what God gives*—even when he didn't understand it.

God did not choose to reveal everything to Job. He doesn't reveal everything to us, either. And the truth is, he doesn't have to. He is God. He is Creator and we are the created. God does not owe us an explanation.

And what if God had spelled it out? What if he had

explained his full plan and purpose for Job's suffering? We tend to think that if we only knew why we were suffering, we would be able to bear it. But would we?

Somehow I think that even if God listed all the reasons he has allowed you to lose your loved one, develop the disease, or suffer the rejection, it still wouldn't seem worth it from your limited perspective. Instead, he expands our perspective by giving us a glimpse of his ability to run the universe in contrast to our limited understanding and experience.

Job had no idea that he was a player in a cosmic confrontation. As we read the ancient story, we are privy to the deal made between God and Satan, but Job had no such context for his suffering. He had no idea that his faithfulness in extreme difficulty mattered so much. But it did. Job teaches us that *our* response to testing matters too. Like Job, we often cannot see the hidden purposes of God. Still, we can determine to be faithful and keep walking toward him in the darkness.

Our task is not to decipher exactly how all of life's pieces fit and what they all mean but to remain faithful and obedient to God, who knows all mysteries. That is the kind of faith that is pleasing to God—a faith that is determined to trust him when he has not answered all the questions, when we have not heard the voice from the whirlwind.

Would you be still and listen for the voice of God speaking to you through his Word, perhaps not answering the question "Why?" but revealing the all-important "Who?"

Would you rest in knowing that there are mysteries we will never understand completely in this life, and would you resist trying to explain an unexplainable God?

Would you choose to trust God and continue believing he has a plan and a purpose, even though the future looks dark?

THEN Job replied to the Lord:

"I know that you can do anything, and no one can stop you. You ask, 'Who is this that questions my wisdom with such ignorance?' It is I. And I was talking about things I did not understand, things far too wonderful for me.

"You said, 'Listen and I will speak! I have some questions for you, and you must answer them.'"

JOB 42:1-4

SUBMISSION

When Hope was a month or so old, the secretary from church called and told me that we were on the prayer list that went out to church members. They were asking people to pray that God would work a miracle and heal Hope. I told her, "That is not how we feel led to pray." We didn't ask God for that. It didn't seem right. Or maybe we were afraid to pray that, to expect that, when the diagnosis seemed so sure and so grim.[13]

In those early weeks, God seemed to speak to me clearly—though not in an audible voice. I've never heard that. He spoke to me through Scripture.

In my Bible study a couple of weeks after Hope was born, we looked at the story of Hagar, who had run away from Abram and Sarai due to Sarai's harsh treatment. Hagar wanted to escape her difficult situation, but God spoke to her in the desert, telling her to "return . . . and submit" (Genesis 16:9). My Bible-study leader asked, "What is God calling you to submit to?" I knew God was calling me to submit to the journey we were facing with Hope—not to fight it or to cry out to him to change it, but to submit to his plan and his purposes.

At the same time, we were talking in Sunday school about the biblical account of the angel who came to Mary to tell her that she would give birth to a son. How did this "favored" one respond? "I am the Lord's servant. . . . May it be to me as you have said" (Luke 1:38, NIV). Mary submitted, even though what God had brought into her life, from her perspective as a thirteen-year-old Jewish maiden, must have looked like a disaster.

Once again, I sensed a calling to submit to the plan God had laid out before us and to walk through it in a way that would bring him glory, a way that would exemplify what it means to trust him in the midst of sorrow and difficulty and disappointment.

For me, submission has meant a quiet, though sorrowful, acceptance of God's plan and God's timing. It has meant giving up the plans I had for my daughter, for my family, for my life, and bringing them all under submission to God.

I wish that it had been a onetime decision, a onetime sacrifice. But throughout Hope's life, as her condition slowly deteriorated, in the days of grief that have followed her death, and as we've walked through nine long months of this new pregnancy, the call to submission hasn't stopped, and it hasn't gotten easier. Every day, as I let go of my dreams and my desires, as I see little girls the age Hope would have been bringing a smile to the faces of their moms and dads, as I plan for another child who will only be with us for a short time, I'm once again called upon to submit. Some days I do better than others.

But because I believe God's plans for me are better than what I could plan for myself, rather than run away from the path he has set before me, I want to run toward it. I don't want to try to change God's mind—his thoughts are perfect. I want to think his thoughts. I don't want to change God's timing—his timing is perfect. I want the grace to accept his timing. I don't want to change God's plan—his plan is perfect. I want to embrace his plan and see how he is glorified through it. I want to submit.

I know that it has been difficult for many people around us to understand why we have not cried out to heaven for healing. Is it because we think that it is too hard for God? Absolutely not. God can do anything.

Often, I see the body of Christ put so much into pursuing God for healing. With great boldness and passion and persistence, we cry out to God, begging for physical healing. And in these prayers, there is often a tiny P.S. added at the end where we say, "If it be your will."

But shouldn't we switch that around?

Shouldn't we cry out to God with boldness and passion and persistence in a prayer that says, "God, would you please accomplish your will? Would you give me a willing heart to embrace *your* plan and *your* purpose? Would you mold me into a vessel that you can use to accomplish what you have in mind?" And then, perhaps, we could add a tiny P.S. that says, "If that includes healing, we will be grateful."

Isn't real faith revealed more through pursuing God and what he wants than through pursuing what we want?

At the end of Job's story, we begin to catch a glimpse of how God used the pain in Job's life. I think this is the same thing God wants to do with the pain you and I experience in life.

After all the crying, after all the questioning, God revealed himself as sovereign over all Creation, and Job recognized God's authority over the universe and God's authority in his life. He came to a place of submission to God's sovereignty.

If we want to find our way to the heart of God on the pathway of suffering, we, too, must submit to the sovereignty of God, saying, in effect, "Yes, sir. You are in charge. I'm yours. You can do anything you want to do."

Jesus himself is the perfect example of submission. In Philippians 2, Paul tells us:

> *Your attitude should be the same that Christ Jesus had. Though he was God, he did not demand and cling to his rights as God. He*

made himself nothing; he took the humble
position of a slave and appeared in human form.
And in human form he obediently humbled
himself even further by dying a criminal's death
on a cross.

PHILIPPIANS 2:5-8

We often hear people talk about the "victorious Christian life." But isn't the life of a Christian really more about bending the knee, humbling ourselves, and taking up a cross? Jesus said it is.

If any of you wants to be my follower, you must
put aside your selfish ambition, shoulder your
cross, and follow me.

MATTHEW 16:24

I don't know what the cross will look like for you. I just know it will require a death to your desires and your dreams to carry it. And I know it won't be easy.

But I also know that as you die to yourself, God's life will take root and grow within you. And as you die to your dreams, his dream can flourish.

Submission to God's sovereignty means bowing the knee whether or not we understand, whether or not we have it figured out, whether or not we agree. In that submission, we find the strength and grace to keep going. We even find joy in the journey.

I was right when I told our pastor that this is where the rubber meets the road—the place where I discover if I really believe what I say I believe. And I have. Like Job, I have come to a place of submission to God's sovereignty. I don't just say I believe in God's sovereignty; I *really* believe it. I believe that God brought David and me, with our recessive gene for Zellweger, together, and that long ago he knew we would have a beautiful daughter named Hope. He knew that she would have a short but purpose-filled life. And if I can trust him with all the things he has brought into my life that I would label as "good," I can trust him with this, too, knowing that his purposes are for my ultimate good.

When we come to these hard places, we discover the real benefit of walking with God and pursuing an intimate relationship with him when there is no tragedy driving us to him. You see, when we know God, when we know his character by studying his Word, we can trust him. We don't resent his sovereignty, his authority, his plan. We can embrace it. We can rest in it.

What is God calling you to submit to today? Is it a difficult situation, a demanding person, an unfulfilled dream, a separation, a limitation, a loss? Are you willing to submit?

Would you examine your heart and life for areas you have not yet given over to the authority of God?

Would you begin today to get to know God better through his Word so that you can rest in his sovereignty as well as his love for you?

Submission

Our Father in heaven, may your name be honored. May your Kingdom come soon. May your will be done here on earth, just as it is in heaven.

MATTHEW 6:9-10

"I had heard about you before, but now I have seen you with my own eyes. I take back everything I said, and I sit in dust and ashes to show my repentance." . . .

So the Lord blessed Job in the second half of his life even more than in the beginning. For now he had fourteen thousand sheep, six thousand camels, one thousand teams of oxen, and one thousand female donkeys. He also gave Job seven more sons and three more daughters. . . .

Job lived 140 years after that, living to see four generations of his children and grandchildren. Then he died, an old man who had lived a long, good life.

JOB 42:5-6, 12-13, 16-17

INTIMACY

So we've come to the end of Job's story. And perhaps you are wondering if it was all worth it for Job. You're probably also wondering if all of your suffering has been worth what it has cost you. There's only one thing that could make it worth it for you. It is the one thing that I'm counting on as I say yes to the suffering God has allowed and is allowing in my life—the same thing that made it worth it for Job.

Job's life as he knew it had ended. His property had been destroyed, his children had died, and he was still covered with scabs. He had been to the depths, craving death, craving answers, craving restoration. His wife and his friends had provided no comfort.

But finally God spoke, and as God revealed himself in the whirlwind, Job realized that even though he had feared and followed God, he hadn't really known God. Through suffering, however, God had revealed himself to Job in an unmistakable, intimate way. Job recognized that though he had known much about God before, he now knew God in a new, more meaningful way that would transform the remainder of his life.

When Job said, "I had heard about you before, but now I have seen you with my own eyes," he was saying, "I knew about you, but I only knew you by the book. Now I know you because I've *experienced* you for myself! This is not just reading about or hearing about you; now I really know you!"

It is one thing to believe that God is faithful and will supply all your needs—even in the darkest of times. It is another thing to *experience* it. In the darkest of days, we've experienced a supernatural strength and peace that could only come from God. Perhaps you have too.

My husband tends to be a pessimist. Not only does he see the glass as half-empty, he's sure what's left is going to spill all over the place any minute. David says he has always feared a tragedy in his life.

But he says that now that the tragedy has come, the fear is gone. Now that he has experienced his greatest fear, and experienced God's supreme faithfulness to us through this difficulty, he no longer fears tragedy in our lives. We know God more fully because we've experienced him more fully through our sorrow.

The apostle Paul also experienced what it was like to go from knowing *about* God to *knowing* God. Knowing God, developing an intimate relationship

with him, became the focus of his life and gave purpose to his suffering. In his letter to the Philippians,
Paul wrote:

> *Yes, everything else is worthless when compared
> with the priceless gain of knowing Christ
> Jesus my Lord. I have discarded everything
> else, counting it all as garbage, so that I may
> have Christ and become one with him. . . .
> As a result, I can really know Christ and
> experience the mighty power that raised him
> from the dead. I can learn what it means to
> suffer with him, sharing in his death, so that,
> somehow, I can experience the resurrection from
> the dead!*

> PHILIPPIANS 3:8-11

Job, like Paul, discovered a new place of intimacy
with God through his severe suffering. And it is
uniquely through suffering that we can find our way
to the very heart of God. In fact, there is no other
pathway that can take us there.

It is when we are hurting the most that we run to
God. We recognize that we are powerless and that he
is powerful. We pray and we see him more clearly because we're desperately looking for him.

And in our looking for him, we find him to be
more loving and faithful than we've ever seen him before. We discover an intimacy that we have never ex-

perienced before, perhaps because we're looking for him so intently. That is always God's purpose: to use whatever means he sees fit to bring us to a closer relationship with him, to create in us a faith that will give us the strength to keep holding on to hope—not a flimsy wishing or a hope that everything will be fixed in this life but genuine biblical hope that one day what is unseen will be seen. This faith is confidence in an eternal future in which God sets everything right.

Was that God's purpose in Job's life, or did he permit all of Job's suffering just to prove to Satan that Job truly did fear God? Was Job a mere pawn in a game between God and Satan?

No. Job's end was better than his beginning, and it wasn't because he was more prosperous materially. It wasn't because he had more children. (I don't think more children could ever have taken away the grief over those ten who were lost.) Job was blessed through his brokenness by his restless pursuit of God. He gained a new, more intimate relationship with God that he never could have found without the pain and sorrow.

And God has the same purpose in mind for you and for me if we will look for him.

To truly discover the heart of God, we need only to look up from our circumstances and look to the Cross. It is there, as we gaze upon our suffering Savior, that we see the Father's heart—a loving Father who "did not spare even his own Son but gave him up for us all" (Romans 8:32). As we gaze upon the Cross and the enormous suffering it represents on our behalf, we recognize that not only does God understand our suffering, but he *chose* to suffer so that he might draw us to himself. "Christ also suffered when he died for our sins once for all time. He never sinned, but he died for sinners that he might bring us safely home to God" (1 Peter 3:18).

Wouldn't you like to come home?

Rather than running from or resenting your suffering, would you be willing to look for God in it?

Would you allow suffering to lead you to the very heart of God, a place where you can find the comfort and peace that you crave as well as the hope that has the power to transform your tomorrows?

God wants to bring you to a place where you can say, "I've not only heard of you, I've seen you! I know you!" And perhaps he has used pain to bring you to that place.

God wants to use the difficulties in your life not to punish you or to hurt you but to draw you to himself.

Will you come?

Come to me, all of you who are weary and carry heavy burdens, and I will give you rest.

MATTHEW 11:28

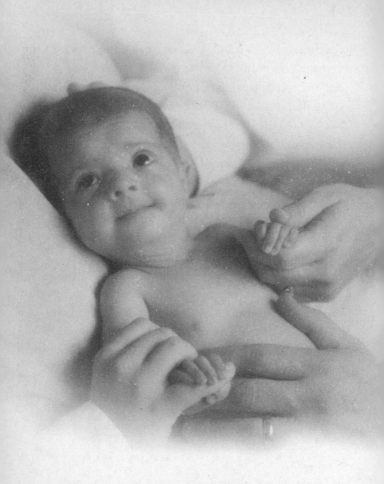

Hope Lauren Guthrie

November 23, 1998–June 9, 1999

Gabriel Johnson Guthrie
July 16, 2001–January 15, 2002

EPILOGUE

> *As I was praying, Gabriel, whom I had seen in
> the earlier vision, came swiftly to me at the time
> of the evening sacrifice. He explained to me,
> "Daniel, I have come here to give you insight
> and understanding."*
>
> DANIEL 9:21-22

On July 16, 2001, we headed to the hospital with several name possibilities for our son to be born that day. I suppose we felt some pressure. We wanted his name to be as significant and meaningful as *Hope* had been for our daughter. And after he was safely delivered, one name easily rose to the top of the list—Gabriel. That day, David sent an e-mail to friends and family that explained our choice. He said:

> *We chose his name because we believe that he,
> like the angel Gabriel, is sent from God, and
> protected by God. We will not be surprised if he
> has heavenly messages for us to hear, if we will
> listen. And significantly, whenever Gabriel
> appeared in the Bible, he reassured his stunned
> audience: "Don't be afraid!"*

Gabriel left us a few days ago, one day short of six months. He seemed stronger than Hope was, and we thought he would be here longer. We spent our days enjoying him and loving him and caring for him, and then he quietly slipped away from us. And once again, we are back to a family of three, with Hope and Gabriel now waiting for us in heaven. As I write, the tears have not yet started. But I know they are coming. At this point, when I think of him, I just smile. What a precious, sweet surprise he was.

And throughout the short six months of his life, we have wondered, *What was his message?*

I suppose there have been many messages. One would have to be: God is in charge of conception. We would like to think that we have the final word on whether we do or do not have a child. Over and over again in Scripture we read that God "closed her womb," God "opened her womb." Now, I don't need anyone to explain the facts of life to me; I understand how this works, but Gabriel's very life said, "God makes babies."

Gabriel, like his sister, Hope, told us that the significance of a life is not measured by its length or by what a person can accomplish or contribute. Gabriel said, "Children are a blessing from the Lord." That blessing comes in different forms—some joyful, some frustrating, some disappointing, some charming, some disarming, some expected, some unexpected—but all a blessing.

Gabriel told us that God uses the weak things of the world to shame the strong (1 Corinthians 1:27, NIV). He showed us that God could use a child who could not see or hear or speak to communicate the most important truths of the universe to the entire world.* If God can do that, perhaps he can use you and me to accomplish his purposes in our corner of the world if we yield ourselves to him.

But I think there is one message that is supreme. It is the same message the angel Gabriel brought the three times he appeared in the Bible.

In the Old Testament book of Daniel, God sent the angel Gabriel, instructing him to explain to Daniel the meaning of a vision. Gabriel said to Daniel, "I have come here to give you insight and understanding" (Daniel 9:22). Gabriel explained the imagery in the dream and the future restoration of God's people, which included the coming of the "Anointed One"— Jesus.

Then, in Luke 1, Gabriel came to Zechariah, an elderly priest in the temple, telling him that his wife would bear a son, John, who would "precede the coming of the Lord, preparing the people for his arrival" (Luke 1:17).

And again in Luke 1, God sends the angel Gabriel

---

*Hope and Gabriel's story was published in the July 16, 2001, issue of *Time* magazine in a story titled, "When God Hides His Face: Can faith survive when hope has died? The Guthries think so," by David Van Biema. The story was republished in numerous newspapers, on numerous Web sites, and in the various international editions of *Time*.

to Mary, telling her that she would have a son, Jesus, who would be "very great and will be called the Son of the Most High" (Luke 1:32).

Gabriel's message is always the same. It's Jesus. "Don't be afraid, Jesus is coming." For Daniel and his people, held captive in a godless land, hope was found in the revelation that Jesus was coming. For Zechariah and his wife, Elizabeth, disappointed and disgraced by life, hope came in the angel's promise that Jesus was coming. And for Mary, confused, disturbed, and frightened about the future, hope filled her with the holy confidence that Jesus was coming.

And for you and me, as we seek to find God in the midst of our pain, the message is the same—Jesus. Don't be afraid as you face the future. Jesus is coming.

I suppose some had hoped for some supernatural message from our little angel, Gabriel—perhaps something we'd never heard before. God does have a message for us. And because it was so important that you and I get the message, he sent more than an angel, or a baby. He sent his very own Son. John tells us:

> *The Word* [his message] *became flesh and made his dwelling among us. We have seen his glory, the glory of the One and Only, who came from the Father, full of grace and truth.*

> JOHN 1:14 (NIV)

We have the entire message, *everything* God wants us to know, in the person and work of Jesus Christ. Jesus himself is the ultimate articulation of God's love for you and for me. Nothing else is needed. He is the Alpha and Omega, the beginning and the end. Jesus is everything God wants to say to us.

Now, I know that to some, that message may sound very simplistic. "I've heard it before," you might say. And perhaps it seems irrelevant to you and your life. But I have to tell you. At this point, I'm not interested in going through the motions. I'm not interested in writing about or grabbing on to anything that is not real and relevant. My friend, Jesus is real and relevant. And he is essential to having genuine hope to hold on to when you have buried a son that you love—or any other time, for that matter.

"But," you say, "is he really necessary?"

Gabriel came along with David and me on a trip to New York in December. I was working with Anne Graham Lotz on a series of media interviews to promote her new book, *Heaven: My Father's House*. We were in a hotel bar having an interview with a writer who had a lot of good questions, some hard questions. Anne had some fabulous answers that I will never forget.

We were discussing all of the people who perished in the World Trade Center and Pentagon on September 11, and the author asked if those people went to heaven if they were good people. Anne answered his question with a question, saying, "How good would you have to be?"

Good question.

The truth is, none of us are "good enough." The book of Romans tells us:

> *For no one can ever be made right in God's sight by doing what his law commands. For the more we know God's law, the clearer it becomes that we aren't obeying it.*
>
> *We are made right in God's sight when we trust in Jesus Christ to take away our sins. And we all can be saved in this same way, no matter who we are or what we have done.*
>
> ROMANS 3:20, 22

The interviewer asked Anne, "But what about those of other faiths in the towers? Aren't there many ways to God?"

Anne said, "I think if there had been any other way, he wouldn't have sent his Son to die."

That makes sense if you think about it, doesn't it? If sincerity, no matter what you believed sincerely, were enough, then there would have been no need for Jesus. If you could get to God just by being a "spiritual" person (whatever that means) or by going to church, then certainly Jesus would not have had to die.

That makes Jesus relevant to you and to me,

doesn't it? That's why the message of Jesus is so important, because there is no other way to have a relationship with God for eternity except through Jesus.

I know that sounds exclusive and narrow and intolerant and perhaps even simpleminded to some. But I'll risk saying it anyway because it's the truth. And if you have missed reckoning with Jesus so far in your life, then, so far, you've missed the very purpose for which you were created. Perhaps you've been distracted by the busyness of life, disappointed by the hurts of life, or perhaps it is doubt or disillusionment with organized religion that has kept you from Jesus. Most likely it is your pride or your unwillingness to admit that you are a sinner who needs a Savior, or the fear of stepping out to make such a decision to change.

Don't let anything or anyone cause you to miss the message!

Another angel is coming with a message. Next time, it won't be the angel Gabriel; it will be the archangel Michael. Here's what the apostle Paul tells us about that day:

> *I can tell you this directly from the Lord: We who are still living when the Lord returns will not rise to meet him ahead of those who are in their graves. For the Lord himself will come down from heaven with a commanding shout, with the call of the archangel, and with the*

*trumpet call of God. First, all the Christians
who have died will rise from their graves. Then,
together with them, we who are still alive and
remain on the earth will be caught up in the
clouds to meet the Lord in the air and remain
with him forever. So comfort and encourage each
other with these words.*

1 THESSALONIANS 4:15-18

Once again, an angel will come with a message. And once again, the message will be, "Don't be afraid. Jesus is coming!"

Today, would you hear and receive Gabriel's message—Jesus—so you will be ready for that day?

Do you want to draw close to God in the midst of your suffering? Have you heard God's invitation to draw close but are not sure how to accept his invitation? Could it be because you've never accepted God's invitation to know him personally through his Son, Jesus Christ?

Hear and receive Gabriel's message—Jesus.

If you have never taken the first step toward intimacy with God by embracing Jesus, his Son, you can do it right now.

*For if you confess with your mouth that Jesus is
Lord and believe in your heart that God raised
him from the dead, you will be saved. For it is
by believing in your heart that you are made
right with God, and it is by confessing with your*

mouth that you are saved. As the Scriptures
tell us, "Anyone who believes in him will not be
disappointed. . . . Anyone who calls on the name
of the Lord will be saved."

ROMANS 10:9-11, 13

Do you want to call on the name of the Lord right
now? You can do that by praying a simple prayer like
this:

Dear God,

I have heard about you, but now I want to
know you for myself. I want to know for sure
that I am a part of your family and that I will
spend eternity with you. So right now, I accept
your invitation to know you in an intimate
way by inviting you into my life. I recognize
that I am a sinner and unable to save myself. I
believe Jesus died on the cross to take away my
sins and that Jesus rose up from the dead to give
me eternal life. I accept Jesus' sacrifice on my
behalf. Would you now come into my life and
take control of it? I want to spend the rest of my
life knowing and serving you.

Amen.

I would love to hear how God has used Hope and
Gabriel in your life. Write to me at:

Nancy Guthrie
904 Little Bridge Place
Nashville, TN 37221

Visit my Web site at www.nancyguthrie.com to write
a message, read articles about my family, find information on other resources, or request information on
my speaking.

SCRIPTURE RESOURCES

LOSS

When you go through deep waters and great trouble, I will be with you. When you go through rivers of difficulty, you will not drown! When you walk through the fire of oppression, you will not be burned up; the flames will not consume you. (Isaiah 43:2)

God is our refuge and strength, always ready to help in times of trouble. (Psalm 46:1)

He heals the brokenhearted, binding up their wounds. (Psalm 147:3)

For he understands how weak we are; he knows we are only dust. Our days on earth are like grass; like wildflowers, we bloom and die. The wind blows, and we are gone—as though we had never been here. (Psalm 103:14-16)

For he gives his sunlight to both the evil and the good, and he sends rain on the just and on the unjust, too. (Matthew 5:45)

I have told you all this so that you may have peace in me. Here on earth you will have many trials and sorrows. But take heart, because I have overcome the world. (John 16:33)

If any of you wants to be my follower, you must put aside your selfish ambition, shoulder your cross daily, and follow me. If you try to keep your life for yourself, you will lose it. But if you give up your life for me, you will find true life. And how do you benefit if you gain the whole world but lose or forfeit your own soul in the process? (Luke 9:23-25)

Anyone who listens to my teaching and obeys me is wise, like a person who builds a house on solid rock. Though the rain comes in torrents and the floodwaters rise and the winds beat against that house, it won't collapse, because it is built on rock. But anyone who hears my teaching and ignores it is foolish, like a person who builds a house on sand. When the rains and floods come and the winds beat against that house, it will fall with a mighty crash. (Matthew 7:24-27)

But to keep me from getting puffed up, I was given a thorn in my flesh, a messenger from Satan to torment me and keep me from getting proud. Three different times I begged the Lord to take it away. Each time he said, "My gracious favor is all you need. My power works best in your weakness." So now I am glad to boast about my weaknesses, so that the power of Christ may work through me. Since I know it is all for Christ's good, I am quite content with my weaknesses and with insults, hardships, persecutions, and calamities. For when I am weak, then I am strong. (2 Corinthians 12:7-10)

Can anything ever separate us from Christ's love? Does it mean he no longer loves us if we have trouble or calamity, or are persecuted, or are hungry or cold or in danger or threatened with death? (Even the Scriptures say, "For your sake we are killed every day; we are being slaughtered like sheep.") No, despite all these things, overwhelming victory is ours through Christ, who loved us. And I am convinced that nothing can ever separate us from his love. Death can't, and life can't. The angels can't, and the demons can't. Our fears for today, our worries about tomorrow, and even the powers of hell can't keep God's love away. Whether we are high above the sky or in the deepest ocean, nothing in all creation will ever be able to separate us from the love of God that is revealed in Christ Jesus our Lord. (Romans 8:35-39)

TEARS

You keep track of all my sorrows. You have collected all my tears in your bottle. You have recorded each one in your book. (Psalm 56:8)

I weep with grief; encourage me by your word. Keep me from lying to myself; give me the privilege of knowing your law. I have chosen to be faithful; I have determined to live by your laws. I cling to your decrees. Lord, don't let me be put to shame! If you will help me, I will run to follow your commands. (Psalm 119:28-32)

He was despised and rejected—a man of sorrows, acquainted with bitterest grief. We turned our backs on him and looked the other way when he went by. He was despised, and we did not care. Yet it was our weaknesses he carried; it was our sorrows that weighed him down. And we thought his troubles were a punishment from God for his own sins! But he was wounded and crushed for our sins. He was beaten that we might have peace. He was whipped, and we were healed! (Isaiah 53:3-5)

For the Lord does not abandon anyone forever. Though he brings grief, he also shows compassion according to the greatness of his unfailing love. For he does not enjoy hurting people or causing them sorrow. (Lamentations 3:31-33)

In that day he will remove the cloud of gloom, the shadow of death that hangs over the earth. He will swallow up death forever! The Sovereign Lord will wipe away all tears. (Isaiah 25:7-8)

He will remove all of their sorrows, and there will be no more death or sorrow or crying or pain. For the old world and its evils are gone forever. (Revelation 21:4)

WORSHIP

Even though the fig trees have no blossoms, and there are no grapes on the vine; even though the olive crop fails, and the fields lie empty and barren; even though the flocks die in the fields, and the cattle barns are empty, yet I will rejoice in the Lord! I will be joyful in the God of my salvation. (Habakkuk 3:17-18)

But the king replied to Araunah, "No, I insist on buying it, for I cannot present burnt offerings to the Lord my God that have cost me nothing." So David paid him fifty pieces of silver for the threshing floor and the oxen. (2 Samuel 24:24)

Since we are receiving a Kingdom that cannot be destroyed, let us be thankful and please God by worshiping him with holy fear and awe. For our God is a consuming fire. (Hebrews 12:28-29)

For God is Spirit, so those who worship him must worship in spirit and in truth. (John 4:24)

Through each day the LORD pours his unfailing love upon me, and through each night I sing his songs, praying to God who gives me life. (Psalm 42:8)

Your unfailing love is better to me than life itself; how I praise you! (Psalm 63:3)

And they sang in a mighty chorus: "The Lamb is worthy—the Lamb who was killed. He is worthy to receive power and riches and wisdom and strength and honor and glory and blessing." (Revelation 5:12)

GRATITUDE

But giving thanks is a sacrifice that truly honors me. If you keep to my path, I will reveal to you the salvation of God. (Psalm 50:23)

Let your roots grow down into him and draw up nourishment from him, so you will grow in faith, strong and vigorous in the truth you were taught. Let your lives overflow with thanksgiving for all he has done. (Colossians 2:7)

Don't worry about anything; instead, pray about everything. Tell God what you need, and thank him for all he has done. If you do this, you will experience God's peace, which is far more wonderful than the human mind can understand. His peace will guard your hearts and minds as you live in Christ Jesus. . . . I know how to live on almost nothing or with everything. I have learned the secret of living in every situation, whether it is with a full stomach or empty, with plenty or little. For I can do everything with the help of Christ who gives me the strength I need. (Philippians 4:6-7, 12-13)

And as God's grace brings more and more people to Christ, there will be great thanksgiving, and God will receive more and more glory. . . . So we don't look at the troubles we can see right now; rather, we look forward to what we have not yet seen. For the troubles we see will soon be over, but the joys to come will last forever. (2 Corinthians 4:15, 18)

BLAME

Yes, it was God who sent me here, not you! And he has made me a counselor to Pharaoh—manager of his entire household and ruler over all Egypt. (Genesis 45:8)

But the Lord watches over those who fear him, those who rely on his unfailing love. . . . Let your unfailing love surround us, Lord, for our hope is in you alone. (Psalm 33:18, 22)

Fear God and obey his commands, for this is the duty of every person. (Ecclesiastes 12:13)

Don't be afraid of those who want to kill you. They can only kill your body; they cannot touch your soul. Fear only God, who can destroy both soul and body in hell. (Matthew 10:28)

In the same way, it is not my heavenly Father's will that even one of these little ones should perish. (Matthew 18:14)

And this is the will of God, that I should not lose even one of all those he has given me, but that I should raise them to eternal life at the last day. For it is my Father's will that all who see his Son and believe in him should have eternal life—that I should raise them at the last day. (John 6:39-40)

For God so loved the world that he gave his only Son, so that everyone who believes in him will not perish but have eternal life. God did not send his Son into the world to condemn it, but to save it. (John 3:16-17)

SUFFERING

Dear friends, don't be surprised at the fiery trials you are going through, as if something strange were happening to you. Instead, be very glad—because these trials will make you partners with Christ in his suffering, and afterward you will have the wonderful joy of sharing his glory when it is displayed to all the world. . . . So if you are suffering according to God's will, keep on doing what is right, and trust yourself to the God who made you, for he will never fail you. (1 Peter 4:12-13, 19)

This suffering is all part of what God has called you to. Christ, who suffered for you, is your example. Follow in his steps. He never sinned, and he never deceived anyone. He did not retaliate when he was insulted. When he suffered, he did not threaten to get even. He left his case in the hands of God, who always judges fairly. (1 Peter 2:21-23)

Through suffering, these bodies of ours constantly share in the death of Jesus so that the life of Jesus may also be seen in our bodies. . . . That is why we never give up. Though our bodies are dying, our spirits are being renewed every day. For our present troubles are quite small and won't last very long. Yet they produce for us an immeasurably great glory that will last forever! So we don't look at the troubles we can see right now; rather, we look forward to what we have not yet seen. For the troubles we see will soon be over, but the joys to come will last forever. (2 Corinthians 4:10, 16-18)

And since we are his children, we will share his treasures—for everything God gives to his Son, Christ, is ours, too. But if we are to share his glory, we must also share his suffering. Yet what we suffer now is nothing compared to the glory he will give us later. (Romans 8:17-18)

DESPAIR

Day and night, I have only tears for food, while my enemies continually taunt me, saying, "Where is this God of yours?" My heart is breaking as I remember how it used to be: I walked among the crowds of worshipers, leading a great procession to the house of God, singing for joy and giving thanks—it was the sound of a great celebration! Why am I discouraged? Why so sad? I will put my hope in God! I will praise him again—my Savior and my God! (Psalm 42:3-6)

Whom have I in heaven but you? I desire you more than anything on earth. My health may fail, and my spirit may grow weak, but God remains the strength of my heart; he is mine forever. (Psalm 73:25-26)

Yet I still dare to hope when I remember this: . . . I say to myself, "The Lord is my inheritance; therefore, I will hope in him!" . . . So it is good to wait quietly for salvation from the Lord. (Lamentations 3:21, 24, 26)

WHY?

We can rejoice, too, when we run into problems and trials, for we know that they are good for us—they help us learn to endure. And endurance develops strength of character in us, and character strengthens our confident expectation of salvation. (Romans 5:3-4)

And we know that God causes everything to work together for the good of those who love God and are called according to his purpose for them. (Romans 8:28)

And all of us have had that veil removed so that we can be mirrors that brightly reflect the glory of the Lord. And as the Spirit of the Lord works within us, we become more and more like him and reflect his glory even more. (2 Corinthians 3:18)

We are pressed on every side by troubles, but we are not crushed and broken. We are perplexed, but we don't give up and quit. We are hunted down, but God never abandons us. We get knocked down, but we get up again and keep going. Through suffering, these bodies of ours constantly share in the death of Jesus so that the life of Jesus may also be seen in our bodies. (2 Corinthians 4:8-10)

So we are always confident, even though we know that as long as we live in these bodies we are not at home with the Lord. That is why we live by believing and not by seeing. Yes, we are fully confident, and we would rather be away from these bodies, for then we will be at home with the Lord. So our aim is to please him always, whether we are here in this body or away from this body. (2 Corinthians 5:6-9)

These trials are only to test your faith, to show that it is strong and pure. It is being tested as fire tests and purifies gold—and your faith is far more precious to God than mere gold. So if your faith remains strong after being tried by fiery trials, it will bring you much praise and glory and honor on the day when Jesus Christ is revealed to the whole world. (1 Peter 1:7)

ETERNITY

David replied, "I fasted and wept while the child was alive, for I said, 'Perhaps the Lord will be gracious to me and let the child live.' But why should I fast when he is dead? Can I bring him back again? I will go to him one day, but he cannot return to me." (2 Samuel 12:22-23)

God has made everything beautiful for its own time. He has planted eternity in the human heart, but even so, people cannot see the whole scope of God's work from beginning to end. (Ecclesiastes 3:11)

He will swallow up death forever! The Sovereign Lord will wipe away all tears. He will remove forever all insults and mockery against his land and people. The Lord has spoken! (Isaiah 25:8)

I assure you, those who listen to my message and believe in God who sent me have eternal life. They will never be condemned for their sins, but they have already passed from death into life. (John 5:24)

But we are citizens of heaven, where the Lord Jesus Christ lives. And we are eagerly waiting for him to return as our Savior. He will take these weak mortal bodies of ours and change them into glorious bodies like his own, using the same mighty power that he will use to conquer everything, everywhere. (Philippians 3:20-21)

For this world is not our home; we are looking forward to our city in heaven, which is yet to come. (Hebrews 13:14)

Blessed and holy are those who share in the first resurrection. For them the second death holds no power, but they will be priests of God and of Christ and will reign with him a thousand years. (Revelation 20:6)

For our perishable earthly bodies must be transformed into heavenly bodies that will never die. When this happens—when our perishable earthly bodies have been transformed into heavenly bodies that will never die—then at last the Scriptures will come true. (1 Corinthians 15:53-54)

For we know that when this earthly tent we live in is taken down—when we die and leave these bodies—we will have a home in heaven, an eternal body made for us by God himself and not by human hands. (2 Corinthians 5:1)

Jesus told her, "I am the resurrection and the life. Those who believe in me, even though they die like everyone else, will live again. They are given eternal life for believing in me and will never perish." (John 11:25-26)

COMFORTERS

Even when I walk through the dark valley of death, I will not be afraid, for you are close beside me. Your rod and your staff protect and comfort me. (Psalm 23:4)

In his kindness God called you to his eternal glory by means of Jesus Christ. After you have suffered a little while, he will restore, support, and strengthen you, and he will place you on a firm foundation. (1 Peter 5:10)

When others are happy, be happy with them. If they are sad, share their sorrow. (Romans 12:15)

Since God chose you to be the holy people whom he loves, you must clothe yourselves with tenderhearted mercy, kindness, humility, gentleness, and patience. You must make allowance for each other's faults and forgive the person who offends you. Remember, the Lord forgave you, so you must forgive others. (Colossians 3:12-13)

Be kind to each other, tenderhearted, forgiving one another, just as God through Christ has forgiven you. (Ephesians 4:32)

And here is how to measure it—the greatest love is shown when people lay down their lives for their friends. (John 15:13)

MYSTERY

There are secret things that belong to the Lord our God, but the revealed things belong to us and our descendants forever, so that we may obey these words of the law. (Deuteronomy 29:29)

Oh, what a wonderful God we have! How great are his riches and wisdom and knowledge! How impossible it is for us to understand his decisions and his methods! For who can know what the Lord is thinking? Who knows enough to be his counselor? (Romans 11:33-34)

All these faithful ones died without receiving what God had promised them, but they saw it all from a distance and welcomed the promises of God. They agreed that they were no more than foreigners and nomads here on earth. And obviously people who talk like that are looking forward to a country they can call their own. If they had meant the country they came from, they would have found a way to go back. But they were looking for a better place, a heavenly homeland. That is why God is not ashamed to be called their God, for he has prepared a heavenly city for them. (Hebrews 11:13-16)

But others trusted God and were tortured, preferring to die rather than turn from God and be free. They placed their hope in the resurrection to a better life. (Hebrews 11:35)

To keep me from getting puffed up, I was given a thorn in my flesh, a messenger from Satan to torment me and keep me from getting proud. Three different times I begged the Lord to take it away. Each time he said, "My gracious favor is all you need. My power works best in your weakness." So now I am glad to boast about my weaknesses, so that the power of Christ may work through me. Since I know it is all for Christ's good, I am quite content with my weaknesses and with insults, hardships, persecutions, and calamities. For when I am weak, then I am strong. (2 Corinthians 12:7-10)

People of Israel, listen! . . . With the help of lawless Gentiles, you nailed [Jesus] to the cross and murdered him. However, God released him from the horrors of death and raised him back to life again, for death could not keep him in its grip. (Acts 2:22-24)

We who have fled to him for refuge can take new courage, for we can hold on to his promise with confidence. This confidence is like a strong and trustworthy anchor for our souls. It leads us through the curtain of heaven into God's inner sanctuary. (Hebrews 6:18-19)

What is faith? It is the confident assurance that what we hope for is going to happen. It is the evidence of things we cannot yet see. (Hebrews 11:1)

The righteous pass away; the godly often die before their time. And no one seems to care or wonder why. No one seems to understand that God is protecting them from the evil to come. For the godly who die will rest in peace. (Isaiah 57:1-2)

That is what the Scriptures mean when they say, "No eye has seen, no ear has heard, and no mind has imagined what God has prepared for those who love him." (1 Corinthians 2:9)

SUBMISSION
Shadrach, Meshach, and Abednego replied, "O Nebuchadnezzar, we do not need to defend ourselves before you. If we are thrown into the blazing furnace, the God whom we serve is able to save us. He will rescue us from your power, Your Majesty. But even if he doesn't, Your Majesty can be sure that we will never serve your gods or worship the gold statue you have set up." (Daniel 3:16-18)

But I am trusting you, O Lord, saying, "You are my God!" My future is in your hands. (Psalm 31:14-15)

You have allowed me to suffer much hardship, but you will restore me to life again and lift me up from the depths of the earth. (Psalm 71:20)

I wait quietly before God, for my salvation comes from him. He alone is my rock and my salvation, my fortress where I will never be shaken. (Psalm 62:1-2)

If you refuse to take up your cross and follow me, you are not worthy of being mine. If you cling to your life, you will lose it; but if you give it up for me, you will find it. (Matthew 10:38-39)

He told them, "My soul is crushed with grief to the point of death. Stay here and watch with me." He went on a little farther and fell face down on the ground, praying, "My Father! If it is possible, let this cup of suffering be taken away from me. Yet I want your will, not mine." (Matthew 26:38-39)

He must become greater and greater, and I must become less and less. (John 3:30)

God blesses the people who patiently endure testing. Afterward they will receive the crown of life that God has promised to those who love him. (James 1:12)

While we live, we live to please the Lord. And when we die, we go to be with the Lord. So in life and in death, we belong to the Lord. (Romans 14:8)

But when the Holy Spirit controls our lives, he will produce this kind of fruit in us: love, joy, peace, patience, kindness, goodness, faithfulness, gentleness, and self-control. (Galatians 5:22-23)

The eyes of the Lord search the whole earth in order to strengthen those whose hearts are fully committed to him. (2 Chronicles 16:9)

INTIMACY

This is what the Lord says: "Let not the wise man gloat in his wisdom, or the mighty man in his might, or the rich man in his riches. Let them boast in this alone: that they truly know me and understand that I am the Lord who is just and righteous, whose love is unfailing, and that I delight in these things. I, the Lord, have spoken!" (Jeremiah 9:23-24)

I will walk among you; I will be your God, and you will be my people. (Leviticus 26:12)

You will show me the way of life, granting me the joy of your presence and the pleasures of living with you forever. (Psalm 16:11)

The Lord is a shelter for the oppressed, a refuge in times of trouble. Those who know your name trust in you, for you, O Lord, have never abandoned anyone who searches for you. (Psalm 9:9-10)

Yes, everything else is worthless when compared with the priceless gain of knowing Christ Jesus my Lord. I have discarded everything else, counting it all as garbage, so that I may have Christ and become one with him. I no longer count on my own goodness or my ability to obey God's law, but I trust Christ to save me. For God's way of making us right with himself depends on faith. As a result, I can really know Christ and experience the mighty power that raised him from the dead. I can learn what it means to suffer with him, sharing in his death, so that, somehow, I can experience the resurrection from the dead! (Philippians 3:8-11)

And so, dear brothers and sisters, I plead with you to give your bodies to God. Let them be a living and holy sacrifice—the kind he will accept. When you think of what he has done for you, is this too much to ask? Don't copy the behavior and customs of this world, but let God transform you into a new person by changing the way you think. Then you will know what God wants you to do, and you will know how good and pleasing and perfect his will really is. (Romans 12:1-2)

Because of Christ and our faith in him, we can now come fearlessly into God's presence, assured of his glad welcome. (Ephesians 3:12)

So, you see, it is impossible to please God without faith. Anyone who wants to come to him must believe that there is a God and that he rewards those who sincerely seek him. (Hebrews 11:6)

Since we have a great High Priest who rules over God's people, let us go right into the presence of God, with true hearts fully trusting him. (Hebrews 10:21-22)

In his goodness he chose to make us his own children by giving us his true word. And we, out of all creation, became his choice possession. (James 1:18)

Draw close to God, and God will draw close to you. (James 4:8)

ENDNOTES

[1]Reading from Max Lucado's *The Great House of God* (Dallas: Word Publishing, 1997) taught me the broader picture—that Satan has no power that God does not permit and that God gave Satan the permission and set the parameters for Satan to test Job. This concept is found in chapter 13 of Lucado's book.

[2]In the days following Hope's death, I found great comfort in reading Gregory Floyd's *A Grief Unveiled: One Father's Journey Through the Death of a Child* (Brewster, Ma.: Paraclete Press, 1999). Not only did I find companionship on the path of grief over losing a child, but I also discovered a faithful follower of Christ. I learned from Floyd's example as well as his words. He wrote about his son, and I adapted some of his words: "I realize that sometimes the reason I feel so strange is that part of my heart is not here any more. I gave it to Johnny and he took it with him" (p. 192).

[3]John R. Claypool, *Tracks of a Fellow Struggler* (New Orleans: Insight Press, 1995), 74–75.

[4]I am indebted to Jerry Bridges for his help in understanding what it means to fear God through his book *The Joy of Fearing God* (Colorado Springs, Co.: WaterBrook Press, 1997).

[5]Eugene Peterson, *THE MESSAGE: Job* (Colorado Springs, Co.: NavPress, 1996), 9. I benefited greatly from reading and rereading Eugene Peterson's paraphrase of the book of Job in *THE MESSAGE.* I'm so grateful for *THE MESSAGE,* which made Job come alive to me and

has made many other passages of Scripture so much more meaningful to me as well.

[6]I was working on the publicity for Kay Arthur's *As Silver Refined* (Colorado Springs, Co.: WaterBrook Press, 1997) while I was pregnant with Hope. Kay's teaching on the sovereignty of God and how he uses life's disappointments to refine us prepared me to welcome his work in me and provided insights for this book.

[7]Bob Benson, *He Speaks Softly* (Waco, Tx.: Word Books, 1985), 65.

[8]Philip Yancey, *Disappointment with God* (Grand Rapids, Mi.: Zondervan Publishing House, 1988), 206. I still have a great deal to learn from Philip Yancey's applications of Job's story in *Disappointment with God*—especially his challenge to replace the question "Why?" with "To what end?" His insights into Job's story run throughout this book.

[9]Ibid., 208. I adapted a quote Yancey credited to Rabbi Abraham Heschel that reads, "Faith like Job's cannot be shaken because it is the result of having been shaken."

[10]Claypool, *Tracks of a Fellow Struggler*, 94.

[11]With help from both Philip Yancey, *Disappointment with God*, 190; and Gregory Floyd, *A Grief Unveiled*, 87.

[12]Peterson, *THE MESSAGE: Job*, 6.

[13]Some of the material in this chapter first appeared in print in a magazine article I wrote, entitled "Praying for Hope," which was published in *Christianity Today* (July 9, 2000).

AN INTRODUCTION
TO THIS STUDY GUIDE

This guide has been designed to be used by an individual or group to study the book of Job and its themes. Studying Job is a thrilling but daunting undertaking. Job's story addresses some of the most profound questions of human experience and an all-powerful God. Perhaps the most important lesson of the book of Job is that there are no simplistic answers to these questions—that God, while knowable, is also mysterious.

Like the book of Job itself, this study does not nail down all of the answers to the questions that Job's story raises. But it will help you and those you study with to dig deeply into Scripture to discover more about who God is and how he works in the universe and in us. While he remains a God whose ways are often unexplainable, he has chosen to make himself knowable. That is why he has revealed himself to us through the person and work of Jesus and through the pages of Scripture. He "rewards those who sincerely seek him" (Hebrews 11:6) like Job did—and the reward is himself.

For individual study, this guide provides seven weeks of daily questions that will encourage your own pursuit and understanding of God through the study of his Word. You will study the entire book of Job as well as many other Scripture passages about issues that Job's story raises. And you will be encouraged to apply what you learn to your life so that God might use it to make you more like his Son. And that's a good thing, isn't it? A commitment to the study will help you solidify the life-transforming habit of daily Bible study, as well as build your anticipation for all that God wants to say to you and show you through your reading of the Bible beyond these fifty days.

But don't become discouraged if you fall behind or are

unable to get to the study every day. Just work through the questions as you can, so you will be able to listen to all that God wants to say to you.

For group study, this guide provides questions for a weekly discussion of Job and its themes, as well as daily study assignments that will prepare group members for a meaningful discussion the next week. It also suggests chapters of *Holding on to Hope* that correspond to the passages of Job being studied that week. You may want to select some of the daily study questions from the previous week to add to the group discussion questions as time permits.

If you are leading the group, I encourage you to set a tone of openness, beginning with your first session together, so that everyone feels free to confront the difficult questions raised in Job's story and to share about the hurts in their life. Your group should be a place where hurting people feel accepted and cared for by others. However, you may find it necessary to clarify that the purpose of your group is to study and discuss the Scripture rather than to serve as a support group. You may also want to plan carefully which discussion questions to cover, setting an approximate amount of time for each question so that you are sure to get through all of the topics in the time allotted.

Many of the questions are open-ended and include "What do you think?" Encourage your participants to recognize that those are opinion questions and there may not be a "right" answer. Make your group a safe place to be bold with opinions. At the same time, lean on the revealed truth of God's Word for answers rather than opinions. Encourage group members to support their views with Scripture.

Some days call for reading or skimming large portions of Job. If this is difficult for you, you may choose to read only the portions required for answering the questions. In skimming, you might also rely on the paragraph and section headings to get a feel for the flow and emphasis of the chapter. If your week does not allow you to answer the questions each day, focus on the "Preparing for Discussion" questions at the end of each week so the group discussion will be more meaningful for you.

I also encourage you to become as comfortable as possible with not having to nail down every issue with a black-and-white answer. In truth, there is much we cannot understand about God and much we cannot control in this world. What we can control is how we respond to the circumstances God allows into our lives and how we choose to pursue God in the midst of our questions. Encourage your group members to keep pursuing God with their questions while committing to love, serve, and trust him even if their questions are never answered to their satisfaction.

My prayer in preparing this study has been that God will honor your desire for him, and that this study will not be merely an intellectual pursuit but one that transforms your heart and mind. If you are suffering or are touched deeply by the pain of this world, this study will have special meaning for you. I have tried to include many of the most difficult questions that have pressed in on me in dark places. May God honor the effort you put into this study so that he might fill the dark places in your life with the light of his very presence.

Nancy Guthrie

For other small group resources go to
www.nancyguthrie.com.

CONTENTS &
STUDY SCHEDULE

WEEK 1

Job: History's Most Significant Sufferer

Small Group Discussion Questions

1. What is your impression of Job based on what you already know about him?

2. What questions do you have about Job before we begin our study?

3. What aspects of Job's experience and interaction with God make you most uncomfortable or leave you with significant questions?

4. Most of us are uncomfortable with Job's story because we fear suffering in our own life or because we've experienced significant suffering in our own life. If you feel comfortable doing so, finish this sentence: *The suffering God has allowed into my life includes . . .* or *The suffering that I fear the most is . . .*

5. What do you hope you will gain from investing your time and effort in the group sessions and in the daily Bible study involved with this study of Job?

Daily Study

DAY 1: Read Job 1–2

1. What kind of a person was Job?

2. What was Satan looking for? What do you think he really wanted to do?

3. What was God confident about in regard to Job?

4. What did God give Satan permission to do in this chapter and what happened?

5. If you were in Job's situation, how do you think you might have responded?

DAY 2: Skim Job 3–21

1. What are some phrases that stand out to you that indicate how Job was feeling and what he was thinking?

2. What are some phrases that indicate the primary message of Job's friends?

3. What did Job want most in these chapters?

4. What did Job reveal at the end of chapter 19 that seemed to give him hope in the midst of his utter despair?

5. Reading through these chapters, we see that Job seemed to vacillate between despair and hope. When have you had that same reaction to some of your struggles?

DAY 3: Skim Job 22–37

1. What are some phrases that reveal Job's friends' underlying belief about how God treats the righteous and the unrighteous?

2. What are some statements that they suggest would "fix" Job's suffering?

3. Which of Job's phrases can you particularly relate to?

DAY 4: Read Job 38–41

1. Summarize God's response to Job.

2. What do you learn about suffering and about the reasons and solution for Job's suffering from what God says?

3. As humans, why do you think we have such a craving to know the reasons for suffering?

4. In chapter 40, how did Job respond to God's questions?

DAY 5: Read Job 42

1. Do you think Job was satisfied with God's response to his questions? Why or why not?

2. In what ways did Job's life change because of what he experienced?

3. What questions does this initial reading of the story of Job leave you with about Job, about God, about Satan, and about yourself?

DAY 6: Overview

1. Who are the three main characters in this story (introduced in chapter 1)?

2. What loss invaded Job's life in chapter 1?

3. What happened to Job in chapter 2?

4. In chapters 3–31, Job and his three friends made speeches to each other. Who were these three friends?

5. In chapters 32–37, a fourth friend spoke. What was his name?

6. Who began to speak in chapter 38? What form did his speeches take?

7. How would you summarize what happened in the final chapter of Job (chapter 42)?

Read the corresponding chapters in Holding on to Hope: *Introduction, Loss*

WEEK 2

Job, the Faithful God-Follower; Satan, the Accusing
Alienator; God, the All-Powerful Protector

Small Group Discussion Questions

1. Job is described as "a man of complete integrity"
   (Job 1:1). In what ways is his integrity evident?

2. Often when someone suffers, we say, "She doesn't
   deserve that." What does that statement reveal about
   our assumptions about goodness or godliness in
   relation to suffering?

3. What do you think Satan really wanted? How did
   God's response to Satan (Job 1:12) reveal his
   knowledge of what Satan wanted?

4. What accusation did Satan make against
   Job (1:9-11)? Do you think this is reasonable?

5. God gave Satan permission to harm Job. What does
   this reveal about God? about Satan? about Job?

6. In this challenge, what would define a win for Satan?
   for God? for Job?

7. What aspects of this interchange between God and
   Satan about Job are troubling to you or leave you
   with questions?

8. The book of Job, along with all Scripture, has been
   recorded to reveal to us who God is and how he
   works. What have you learned about God so far in
   this story?

9. How can you apply this truth about God's character
   to a situation in your life?

Daily Study

DAY 1: Job's Life: Before and After
Read chapters 29 and 30 of Job, in which Job describes his life of blessing and honor before the suffering came and the loss and dishonor since the suffering.

1. What are some key phrases that describe Job's character and lifestyle before the suffering?

2. What are some key phrases that describe what life was like for Job after the suffering came?

3. We might expect that when Job was complaining or counting his losses, he would focus on his property, his children, and his health. But what aspects of his life did he mourn the most?

4. Looking back at losses in your life, what aspects of these losses hurt the most?

DAY 2: Satan's Goals and Methods
1. What do the following verses tell you about Satan's goals?

   Mark 4:14-15

   Luke 22:31-32

   1 Thessalonians 2:18

   1 Peter 5:8

2. What do the following verses tell you about Satan's methods of achieving those goals?

   Genesis 3:13

   2 Corinthians 11:14

   2 Thessalonians 2:9

3. How has Satan deceived you in the past?

4. How has Satan tried to take away the seed of God's Word that has been planted in your life?

DAY 3: God's Power, Satan's Power, and Your Power

1. What do the following verses tell you about God's power in relation to Satan's power?

   Luke 4:33-36

   Luke 8:27-33

   1 John 3:8

   Romans 8:38-39

2. What do the following verses tell you about your power over Satan?

   Ephesians 4:27

   Ephesians 6:11

   James 4:7

3. In what day-to-day ways can a person give the devil a foothold in her life?

4. What is one change you could make to keep the devil from having power in your life?

DAY 4: Satan's Ultimate Destiny

1. What do these verses tell you about Satan's ultimate destiny?

   Genesis 3:14-15

   Matthew 25:41

   Romans 16:20

   Revelation 20:1-3, 7-10

2. From these verses, for whom was hell created?

3. What has Satan used to try to drive a wedge between you and God? How can you keep him from being successful?

DAY 5: God's Ultimate Protection

1. Read Psalm 91. How do you respond to God's promise of protection in this psalm? When has this been a reality in your life?

2. Read Matthew 10:28. What does this verse tell you about God's perspective on life and death?

3. Read 1 Thessalonians 5:8-11. What has God ultimately protected us from? For what purpose has God protected us?

4. We have learned that God is more concerned with our souls, which will live forever, than our bodies, which will one day die. How can that knowledge transform your perspective on your current circumstances?

DAY 6: Preparing for Discussion

1. Read Job 1–2 and make notes about specific things Job said or did in response to his loss.

2. Looking at those around you and at your own life, what are typical immediate responses to loss?

3. How do these responses to loss affect us in the long-term?

4. Think about someone you have observed and admired who has faced great difficulty. What did you admire about how he or she responded, and why?

Read the corresponding chapters in Holding on to Hope: *Tears, Worship, Gratitude*

WEEK 3

Job's Initial Response to Loss

Small Group Discussion Questions

1. In what ways did Job show his grief? What are some acceptable and unacceptable ways to show grief in today's culture?

2. What personal experiences have you had with grieving or comforting someone who is grieving that reveal the awkwardness of expressing and consoling grief?

3. Do you find it amazing that Job was able to fall before God in worship at this point in his life? Why? Why do you think he was able to do that?

4. What does it mean to truly worship God? With your possessions? With your abilities? In private? In public? What does a lifestyle of worship look like?

5. Job said, "The Lord gave me everything I had, and the Lord has taken it away" (1:21). How is it possible to be grateful to God when he has given *and* when he has taken away something or someone we love?

6. What does Job's question to his wife, "Should we accept only good things from the hand of God and never anything bad?" (2:10) reveal about Job's attitude toward suffering? What does it reveal about God?

7. Think of individuals from the Old and New Testaments. Discuss the suffering they endured and how they responded to their suffering. (Some ideas include Noah, Abraham, Jacob, Joseph, Moses,

David, Solomon, Jeremiah, Hosea, Mary, John the
Baptist, and Paul.)

8. What assumptions or expectations cause us to be
surprised and offended by suffering in our lives?

Daily Study

DAY 1: Sorrow

1. Read Isaiah 53:3-5 and Matthew 26:36-38. What
does it mean to you that Jesus understands what
sorrow and grief feel like?

2. Read John 11:32-35. Why do you think Jesus wept
even though he knew he was going to raise Lazarus
from the dead?

3. Read Isaiah 25:7-8 and Revelation 21:4. What
promise for the future do you find in both of these
passages?

4. Read 1 Thessalonians 4:13. Speaking to believers,
Paul says that he wants us to know what will happen
to Christians who die so we will not be full of sorrow
like people who have no hope. What do Christians
and non-Christians have in common as they grieve?
What is different about the way they grieve?

5. Read 2 Corinthians 4:8-18. What perspective on his
sorrow enables Paul to write about the future with
joyful anticipation?

6. Take verses 16-18 of 2 Corinthians 4 and write out a
personalized version, changing the "we" to "I" and
including the specific "troubles" you are facing.

DAY 2: Worship

1. Read John 4:23-24. What kind of worshipers does
God seek?

2. What are some ways that we go through the motions of worship rather than worship God "in spirit," or with genuine devotion?

3. In our culture, many people practice a buffet-style religion—they choose which qualities their god possesses, often claiming he's the God of the Bible. How is this different from worshipping God in "truth"?

4. Read 2 Samuel 24:18-25. In this story, King David recognizes that true worship demands sacrifice. What are some of the costs you have paid to worship God sacrificially?

5. This truth is reflected in Romans 12:1, which instructs us to worship God not by offering animals as sacrifices, but by offering ourselves as a living sacrifice. What can you do differently this week to offer yourself as a living sacrifice in worship to God?

DAY 3: Anger

1. Read Psalm 4:4 and Ephesians 4:26. Are feelings of anger inherently sinful? Explain.

2. Read Proverbs 29:11. What do you think it means to give "full vent" to anger?

3. According to Proverbs 29:22, what are some results of giving in to anger and holding on to it?

4. What do you learn about acceptable anger from Mark 3:5 and John 2:13-17?

5. According to James 1:19-20, why should you seek to resist nurturing anger in your life?

DAY 4: Responding to Suffering

1. Read 1 Peter 4. What would it look like for you to "arm [yourself] with the same attitude" (4:1) that Christ had toward suffering?

2. According to verse 19, what should you do if you suffer?

3. According to Romans 5:3-5, how should we respond to suffering and why?

4. As you look back over the suffering you have experienced, how have you responded?

5. The next time suffering comes into your life, how would you like to respond?

DAY 5: Preparing for Discussion, Part 1
Read or skim Job 3–11.

1. Select some of Job's phrases in chapter 3 that best illustrate his state of mind, body, and faith.

2. Perhaps the gist of Eliphaz's entire message can be summed up by his comment in 4:8. Put his message into your own words.

3. What do Eliphaz's words in 5:1 reveal about his own faith and understanding of God?

4. As Job begins to cry out to God in 7:6-21, how does his speech reveal that he does not agree with what Eliphaz said in 5:1?

5. Job's friends say much that is right, good, and true, but it is wrongly applied. Which of their words ring true to you? And yet what is wrong with applying these principles to Job or this circumstance?

6. Job summarizes his complaints against the attitudes and arguments of his friends in 6:26-29. What are they?

7. What does Job long for in 9:32-35 and again in 16:21? How has that longing been fulfilled for us according to 1 Timothy 2:5-6?

8. Zophar is not just blunt but also insulting, and he offers simplistic answers. According to 11:6, what does Zophar imply is the reason for Job's suffering?

DAY 6: Preparing for Discussion, Part 2
Read or skim Job 12–21.

1. Job's response to his friends seems to reject the simplistic view that people bear direct responsibility for everything bad or good that happens to them. What is the cause of suffering Job suggests in chapter 12? What phrases support your answer?

2. What does Job want to do in 13:3? What does this reveal about his faith?

3. Job calls his friends "worthless quacks" in 13:4 and proceeds to list their faults and failures. What criticisms does he name or imply in verses 4, 5, 7, 9, 11, and 12?

4. What is the remedy for death that Job ponders in 14:13-17 and that Jesus declares in John 5:25-29?

5. As Job continues to probe death and beyond, his statements grow bolder. What confidence and hope does he reveal in 19:25-27?

6. How does Job's prophetic description in 19:25-27 relate to 1 Thessalonians 4:16-17 and 1 Corinthians 15:52?

Read the corresponding chapters in Holding on to Hope: *Blame, Suffering*

WEEK 4

Who's to Blame?

Small Group Discussion Questions

1. Beginning in chapter 3, Job is painfully, revealingly honest about his life and his faith, and this can't help but make us uncomfortable. Why do you think we are more comfortable with "tidy" faith than we are with questioning, searching faith? Do you think after Job's initial strong response that his faith has now failed?

2. Amazingly, in chapters 3–37 we don't hear Job complain about losing his children, his servants, his livestock, his property, or his health. What is his essential complaint in 3:25-26? Why do you think we have a tendency to focus our complaints on the specifics of our loss rather than our loss of peace or seeming loss of relationship with God?

3. In what way does Eliphaz sound like a modern name-it-and-claim-it preacher or believer in 5:19-27? How would you refute what he says, and what Scripture would you use?

4. Once again, much of what Job's friends say is right, good, and true, but wrongly applied. While Bildad's words in 8:20 are generally correct, how is this truth misapplied in the case of Job? Can this be applied to Jesus?

5. Job expresses the central question of the book in 9:1-2. What is it?

6. In chapter 9, Job reveals his intense skepticism and feeling of alienation from God. Can a Christian be skeptical and feel alienated from God and still be a Christian? Why is it so difficult and awkward for us to make allowance for confusion, alienation, and oppression in the life of faith?

7. Job expected God would answer and he did, but Job had to wait. What makes waiting to hear from God so difficult?

8. Job's words in 13:15 are a direct answer to the wager between God and Satan that began this drama (Job 1:11). What was the wager, and how was it settled?

9. What good news announced in the New Testament (1 Corinthians 15:54) could have soothed Job's fear and dread of the grave expressed in Job 17:13-16?

10. What difference does the promise of resurrection for the believer make in your heart and mind as you consider those you love who have died? What difference does it make as you consider your own coming death?

Daily Study

DAY 1: The Hand of God

1. In Job 10:8, Job questions God, saying, "You formed me with your hands; you made me, and yet you completely destroy me." What do the following verses in the Psalms reveal about what God does for us with his hands?

Psalm 31:14-15

Psalm 32:4-5

Psalm 75:7-8

Psalm 119:73

Psalm 139:9-10

2. What did Jesus do with his hands, and what does each act mean to you personally?

Mark 8:22-25

Mark 10:16

John 13:3-5

John 20:24-28

DAY 2: Reaping and Sowing

1. Read Job 8:1-7. What does Bildad indicate was the reason for the suffering of Job's children?

2. In Romans 6:22, what is sown and what is reaped?

3. In Romans 6:23, what is earned and what is given instead?

4. In 2 Corinthians 9:6-15, what is sown and what is reaped?

5. Read Galatians 6:7-10. In practical terms, what is the difference between one who sows to please his sinful nature and one who sows to please the Spirit?

6. "Reaping destruction" has both immediate and long-term implications. What sin have you sown that has already resulted in destruction in your life?

7. What have you sown to please the Spirit, and what have you reaped already?

DAY 3: The Curse

1. Read Genesis 3. What curse in each of the following verses is a result of Adam and Eve's sin?

   3:14

   3:15

   3:16

   3:17

   3:19

2. While this passage describes the Curse's effect on the earth and humankind, it also gives us hope for salvation through the seed of the woman—Jesus. How did Satan "strike" Christ's heel? How does Genesis 3:15 relate to Romans 16:20 and Revelation 12:9?

3. Read Romans 8:18-25. What do you learn about the Curse from verses 20 and 21?

4. What does this passage indicate our waiting will be like during this time before the ultimate defeat of Satan and the end of the Curse?

5. In what ways has the Curse impacted your life?

6. What would it mean for you to wait with hope and perseverance?

DAY 4: Is Suffering Punishment for Sin?

1. Read Psalm 103:8-12. What do we deserve and why? What do we receive from God instead?

2. According to Isaiah 53:5-6 and 2 Corinthians 5:21, why did Christ suffer?

3. Read Romans 3:23-26. How are we made right with God?

4. Read Romans 8:1-3. What does it mean to not be condemned, and how is this made possible?

5. According to Hebrews 10:26-31, who will be punished and what will this judgment be like?

6. Have you ever assumed suffering in your life was punishment for something you did or did not do? What do you think now?

DAY 5: Preparing for Discussion, Part 1
Read or skim Job 22–28.

1. According to 22:2-3, how does Eliphaz believe God feels about people?

2. What do Romans 5:8 and 1 Peter 3:18 reveal about the extent to which God cares about us and our righteousness?

3. Read Job's words in 23:8-10 and write your own paraphrase of what Job is expressing.

4. Read Job 23:10 and 1 Peter 1:7. What do these verses say about the trials we face?

5. What parts of Bildad's brief reply do you agree with (chapter 25), and what parts do you disagree with?

6. Read Job 26:1-4. Summarize Job's challenge or question to Bildad.

DAY 6: Preparing for Discussion, Part 2
Read or skim Job 29–37.

1. In chapter 30, Job laments being an outcast and a target of insults. What does Matthew 5:10-12 say to the Christian about how to anticipate being treated by others?

2. What do you see from the prologue in Job 1:1-5 and in the statement in 31:33 that reveal the secret to his blamelessness?

3. After Job's three friends stop talking, the young Elihu begins. What word do you see repeated numerous times in 32:2-5 that gives us a clue to Elihu's disposition and gives context for his words?

4. While Elihu's arguments are not very different from Job's three friends, he suggests that God has a reason or purpose for suffering. What is that purpose in 33:19, 29-30, and 34:10-15?

5. Unlike Job's other three friends, Elihu seems to have some spiritual sensitivity, yet he still condemns Job. In what ways do you see this in yourself as well—even though you love God, you can find yourself judgmental, critical, and unloving toward those around you?

6. Job's plan to wait on God provides the foundation for the saying "the patience of Job." In James 5:11 some translations say that Job "endured patiently" while others commend Job's "perseverance." What does it mean to endure patiently or persevere in the face of suffering?

Read the corresponding chapters in Holding on to Hope: *Despair, Why?*

WEEK 5

Why?

Small Group Discussion Questions

1. For what purpose did God use suffering in the following passages? (You may want to ask various group members to read each of these verses and identify God's purpose in suffering.)

   Psalm 78:34   2 Corinthians 1:3-5

   Proverbs 17:3   2 Corinthians 4:8-10

   Jonah 1:17–2:1   2 Corinthians 12:7

   John 9:1-3   Philippians 1:12-14

   John 15:2   Hebrews 12:10-11

   Romans 5:3-4   James 1:2-4

2. Can you see how God has used suffering in your life or in the life of someone you know for one of these purposes?

3. In chapter 23, while Job expresses his trust in God and his confidence in God's purposes (10-14), he also seems to express terror and dread (15-17). Can a person of faith have confidence in God and still feel terrorized in the midst of trouble?

4. In the middle of Job's ranting, he shares an inspired praise offering in 26:5-14. What does this tell you about his faith and his understanding of God? What does this show you about the relationship between his understanding of God and his questions?

5. Sometimes we aren't willing to cry out to God like Job did in 30:20. What are we afraid of?

6. Job's three friends become frustrated and have nothing more to say. But beginning in chapter 32, Elihu has his turn. Elihu suggests that God has brought suffering into Job's life to discipline him. Even if spiritual discipline was not the primary reason behind Job's suffering, do you think God could have used (or did use) Job's suffering to discipline him?

Daily Study

DAY 1: His Strength in Your Weakness

1. Read 2 Corinthians 12:1-10. Why does Paul say a thorn in the flesh was given to him?

2. Paul calls the thorn "a messenger from Satan" (12:7), yet he seems to indicate that God sent it to him. What might this indicate about God's sovereignty? How does this relate to Job's experience?

3. What do you learn from Paul's example in verse 8?

4. What similarities do you see between Paul's prayer and Jesus' prayer in Mark 14:32-41?

5. How do the Lord's words to Paul encourage you as you apply them to the hurts in your life that at times seem unbearable?

6. What perspective enabled Paul to say that he was glad and content in insults, hardships, persecutions, and calamities (12:9-10)?

7. What weaknesses in your life provide opportunities for God to display his strength? How can you allow him to do that?

Week 5

DAY 2: Spiritual Maturity

1. Read James 1:2-4. What could cause a person to be joyful in the midst of suffering?

2. From verse 4, what response is required in our suffering, and what is the result or reward?

3. What is a mature believer like, according James 2:22 and Ephesians 4:12-16?

4. What is the process for developing spiritual maturity according to 2 Corinthians 3:16-18 and Philippians 3:12-16?

5. Read Hebrews 5:12–6:3. What is it appropriate to expect of a mature believer (v. 12), and what are the evidences of a mature believer (v. 14)?

6. How will you need to adjust your attitude toward suffering to allow it to help you become more spiritually mature?

DAY 3: Genuine Faith Revealed

1. Job 1:12 quotes God as saying to Satan: "All right, you may test him." In what way was Job's suffering a test? What was being tested? For whose benefit was the test?

2. Job seems to recognize that he is being tested, and he does not know about God's statement of confidence in him. What does Job say in 23:10 that he believed was true at the time but came to know by experience through testing?

3. Jesus was put to the ultimate test of the Cross. What does Hebrews 5:7-9 tell us about what was demonstrated in his life?

4. Read 1 Peter 1:6-7. Once again, this writer is suggesting that we have joy in the midst of suffering. What is the source of that joy?

5. Has suffering allowed your faith to be proved genuine? Or has it revealed a lack of faith in your life?

DAY 4: The Glory of God

1. Read Exodus 33:18-23. What did Moses ask God for?

2. What was the essence of God's glory that passed in front of Moses (v. 19)?

3. Read Exodus 34:29-30. How was Moses affected by his exposure to God's glory?

4. Read John 1:14 and Hebrews 1:3. How was God's glory shown in these verses?

5. Read 2 Corinthians 3:13-18. Where is God's glory now seen?

6. Read John 15:8. How do we bring glory to God?

7. What fruit have you produced to the glory of God, or what fruit are you laboring to produce?

DAY 5: Suffering As Discipline

1. Read Hebrews 12:3-11. Recognizing that the writer of Hebrews is speaking to believers who are suffering persecution, what does he say is the intent of God's discipline and who is it for (vv. 5-6)?

2. According to verse 5, what are two ways we can waste God's efforts to discipline us? How should we respond instead, according to verses 9 and 11?

3. Because one of God's attributes is perfection, we know he is the perfect parent. In what ways, then, is his discipline different from that of earthly parents?

4. According to verse 10, what is the goal of God's discipline that assures us it is formative and not punitive?

5. In the same way that any worthy and lofty goal (like losing weight, earning an educational degree, etc.) requires that we endure hardship, submit, and be trained, becoming holy like Jesus will require that you submit to God's discipline. What sacrifices or self-imposed limitations do you think may be required? Are you willing to make these sacrifices?

6. What will be the result or fruit of submitting to God's discipline, according to 12:11?

DAY 6: Preparing for Discussion

1. Read Job 38–41. In 38:1-7, which of his own attributes does God seem to be emphasizing through his questions?

2. Read 40:6-14 and notice words like *justice, judgment, condemn, robes,* and *imprison.* God seems to be responding to Job's challenge to his justice. How does a recognition of God as a perfect and righteous judge impact our tendency to complain that God has not treated us fairly?

3. From 41:11, what is the primary message about God?

4. What is Job's first response to God's revelation? (See Job 40:4.)

5. Put 42:1-2 in your own words—the way you might have said it to God if you were Job.

6. What does Job admit to in 42:3, and what character trait does this confession reflect?

7. What action of Job's is foremost in 42:6? What attitude does this act reveal?

8. What is your understanding of repentance? How is it done, and who needs to repent?

Read the corresponding chapters in Holding on to Hope: *Eternity, Mystery, Submission*

WEEK 6

God Speaks, Job Responds

Small Group Discussion Questions

1. Since God is creator of the universe and creator of everything—including you—what rights or freedoms does that give him?

2. God is a perfect, fair, and righteous judge. What does that mean to you if you are under his rule?

3. If everything under heaven is God's—including you and me—what implications does that have for someone who is demanding that God explain himself?

4. Why do you think God answered Job's and his friends' questions with his own set of questions rather than spelling out the causes and purposes of suffering in general and Job's suffering in particular?

5. How does God's revelation of himself—in the whirlwind to Job, through Jesus, and through Scripture—help us in our quest to make sense of and respond appropriately to suffering?

6. Do you find the idea of submitting to God's sovereignty in your life demanding and scary or freeing? Why?

7. A typical reaction to suffering is a sense of *I don't deserve this!* How would humility change that response?

8. Refer back to your notes from yesterday's question 8. Discuss your understanding of what repentance is, how it is done, and who needs to repent.

Daily Study

DAY 1: Hearing God's Voice

1. God has often spoken through nature like he did in the whirlwind to Job. What did God use and what was his message in the following passages?

   Exodus 3:1-6

   Matthew 17:5

   Romans 1:20

2. According to Hebrews 3:7-15, how should we respond when we hear God's voice?

3. According to these verses, what keeps us from hearing God's voice?

4. What are some ways we harden our hearts?

5. Read Revelation 3:20. What is the promise and who is it made to?

6. What is the condition for the promise (3:19)?

DAY 2: God's Ways and Wisdom

1. As we read Job's story, we are privy to the cosmic confrontation going on between God and Satan, but Job had no such context for his experience. In what way do God's words from the whirlwind in Job 38–41 reflect Zophar's words in Job 11:7?

2. What does Isaiah 55:8-9 mean, and how do you respond to that truth?

Week 6

3. Read Romans 11:33-36. Do you, like Paul, celebrate
   the impossibility of understanding God's decisions
   and methods, or do you find them frustrating and
   defeating? How can you gain a perspective like Paul's,
   enabling you to rejoice in God's unknowable wisdom?

4. While our earthly knowledge and experience limit us,
   what does Ephesians 6:10-12 reveal about happenings
   in the heavenly realms? How is that demonstrated in
   the story of Job?

5. In light of this spiritual dimension, how should you
   respond when you do not understand God's plans,
   purposes, and methods?

DAY 3: Fearing God

1. In 28:28, Job says, "The fear of the Lord is true
   wisdom." In the following verses, what are some traits
   or experiences of those who fear God?

   Job 1:1

   Psalm 25:12-15

   Malachi 3:16-18

   Acts 9:31

   Philippians 2:12-13

2. According to the following verses, what are some
   traits or experiences of those who do not fear God?

   Psalm 36:1-4

   Proverbs 1:7

   Jeremiah 2:19

   Romans 3:10-18

3. Are there any areas of your life—perhaps your speech,
   your habits, your casual attitude toward the things of

God—that reflect a lack of the fear of God in your life? What are they?

4. According to Proverbs 2:1-9, how can you grow in your fear of the Lord?

DAY 4: Humility

1. First Peter 5:5-6 and Colossians 3:12-13 tell us to clothe ourselves with humility. Read those verses and describe how your life would look different than it does now if you were clothed with more humility.

2. How does God reward humility in the following verses?

Psalm 18:27

Psalm 25:9

Psalm 149:4

Proverbs 3:34

Proverbs 11:2

3. Read Matthew 23:11-12. What did Jesus say will happen to the person who is a humble servant?

4. That truth is repeated in James 4:10. How do our pride and our pursuit of looking good in the eyes of others reveal a lack of faith in God's Word?

5. We nurture humility in our lives when we look for opportunities to serve, refuse to seek the spotlight, and purposefully deny our prideful impulses. Think through your schedule and the people you interact with. What can you do—or not do—to nurture a humble spirit in your life?

DAY 5: Repentance

1. Based on Acts 3:19 and Acts 26:20, what action is implied in repentance?

2. According to 2 Corinthians 7:8-11, what is the good result of being made sorry for sin?

3. What is the result of godly sorrow that leads to repentance?

4. According to 2 Peter 3:9, who needs to repent?

5. Repentance is not a one-time experience for the believer, but a part of the process of becoming more pleasing to God as we give more of ourselves to him and are indwelt more fully by the Holy Spirit. What lingering sin do you need to turn away from? What concrete step can you take to turn from that sin?

DAY 6: Preparation for Discussion

1. Read Job 42. What do you think Job means by his statement in verse 5?

2. How do you make sense of what we learned about Job in 1:1 with what we read in 42:5?

3. Thinking back to an earlier discussion about the purpose of suffering and the ways God uses suffering in our lives, what do you think was the purpose in Job's suffering? How did God use it in his life and in the lives of others?

4. What are some things Job's friends said or did that were hurtful to Job?

5. What have some of the "comforters" in your life done right and wrong in the midst of your suffering?

6. Remember how Job wished there could be a mediator between himself and God? In what way does he

become a mediator himself? How do you think that impacted his relationship with his three friends?

7. In 42:7, God says that Job's friends have not been right in what they said about God, like Job was. Do you think everything Job said about God was right? If not, why do you think God was still pleased with Job?

8. From verses 42:10-15, list the ways Job became prosperous again.

9. Do you think the intimacy with God, restored relationships with his friends, and restoration of his prosperity and family made Job's suffering worth all he had been through? Why or why not?

10. Job 42:17 says, "Then he died, an old man who had lived a long, good life." Would you describe Job's life as good? Why or why not?

Read the corresponding chapters in Holding on to Hope: *Comforters, Intimacy*

WEEK 7

The Good Life

Small Group Discussion Questions

1. Throughout most of the book, Job has been full of despair and questions, wishing he had never been born. How did hearing from God change him?

2. Has Job's desire to state his case before God and be judged been fulfilled? At the end of the book, do you think he is left satisfied or unsatisfied?

3. Recognizing that we can never completely understand God's purposes for suffering, in what way did God use Job's suffering for good?

4. How has God used Job's suffering in your life these centuries later? What does this tell you about how your response to suffering (good or bad) could influence those around you and future generations?

5. Just like Job, many of us discover in the midst of loss that our "friends" can often hurt more than help. How has that been true in your life?

6. Why is it so hard to forgive? What does it require? What are the benefits of forgiving those who have hurt us?

7. What are your thoughts about what happens to Job after his suffering—his personal prosperity, new family, and long life?

8. Can all people who stay faithful to God through their suffering assume that God will restore what they have lost in this lifetime? Why or why not?

9. Throughout this drama, Job never knew about the wager between God and Satan. Do you think Job was just an unfortunate victim of this cosmic challenge?

Daily Study

DAY 1: Knowing God

1. Read Philippians 3:1-14. What are some of the things Paul once considered to be advantages that he came to see as disadvantages?

2. If religious works or being a religious "insider" made you right with God, what would you include on your list of advantages? How have these "advantages" helped or hindered you in coming to know God?

3. What perspective and desire did Paul have that moved those advantages from the asset column to the liability column?

4. What things did Paul want most (vv. 10-11)?

5. What do you think Paul means when he says he wants to "learn what it means to suffer with him, sharing in his death" (v. 10)?

6. How has your suffering helped you to know a greater fellowship or intimacy with God? How has it caused you to become like him in his death?

DAY 2: Forgiveness

1. According to each of the following verses, why should we choose to forgive those who hurt us and be reconciled with those we've hurt?

Matthew 5:23-26

Matthew 6:12-15

Colossians 3:12-17

2. How does grasping the enormity of your own sin impact your ability or willingness to forgive others, even when they don't "deserve" it?

3. Forgiveness does not mean making light of what someone has done that hurt you. Instead, it means recognizing the weight of the hurt and refusing to make them pay. Who owes you a debt, and what would it look like for you to mark their debt paid?

4. Sometimes we want others at least to ask forgiveness before we are willing to offer it. What do you learn about this from Jesus' example in Luke 23:33-34?

5. Read Hebrews 12:1-2. Unforgiveness is like a weight that pulls us down as we seek to run the race of faith. How has unforgiveness weighted you down, held you back, or burdened you? What would it be like to be free of that weight?

6. Forgiveness is not a natural reaction but a supernatural one. It may seem like you just do not have the strength to forgive. According to Romans 8:1-11, where can you find the power to forgive those who have hurt you?

DAY 3: Stewardship

1. Read Matthew 25:14-30. What did the master expect of his servants?

2. The servant who delivered five talents and the one who delivered two talents received the same reward. What does this indicate about the master and what pleased him?

3. How do the words of the servant in verses 24-25 remind you of Job's friends' words about God?

4. Why was the servant with one talent judged unfaithful?

5. According to verses 28-30, what happens to those who are faithful and fruitful with what is entrusted to them, and what happens to those who squander what is entrusted to them?

6. What are some of the possessions, opportunities, advantages, experiences, or abilities God has given you that he expects you to be a faithful steward of?

7. Do you want more from God? More resources, more ability, more opportunity? In what ways are you being a good steward of what he has already entrusted to you?

DAY 4: Suffering Redeemed

1. Read Romans 8:28. This is a verse that some of us who have suffered can come to resent as it is quoted "at" us in the midst of grief or loss, and yet its truth brings hope in the midst of despair. Put this verse into your own words.

2. Is this promise universal? If not, for whom is it intended?

3. Joseph understood that God can use even evil for good purposes. How did he express this truth in Genesis 50:20?

4. Does the truth that God causes all things to work together for good mean that all things that happen to us are good? What is the difference?

5. According to Romans 5:3-4, what kind of good can come out of suffering?

6. Have you experienced this good result from suffering
   in your life? Why or why not?

DAY 5: Strength in Suffering

1. Read Psalm 27. What was the one thing David
   wanted most as he faced difficulty in his life?

2. What would it be like for you to "live in the house of
   the Lord," or be at home in God (v. 4)?

3. What are three things this Psalm says that God will do
   (v. 5)?

4. What eight things does David ask God to do in verses
   7-12? Which of these requests would you also ask of
   God?

DAY 6: Preparation for Discussion

1. What are the variations on who seems to be
   responsible for Job's suffering in Job 2:3, 2:7, and
   42:11? How can you reconcile these variations?

2. Read Job 2:10 and Ecclesiastes 7:13-14. What point
   do both references make?

3. What does John 14:28-31 tell you about God's ability
   to use evil to accomplish good?

4. What does Acts 2:22-24 tell you about God's plan?
   What does it tell you about man's responsibility?
   Does the fact that what these wicked men did was
   part of God's eternal plan make what happened
   good?

5. Read Hebrews 5:7-9. How does the fact that Jesus
   struggled with God's plan—which included the pain
   of incurring God's wrath on the cross—help you as
   you struggle with the fact that God's plan for you has
   included suffering?

6. As you consider Jesus on the cross, how do you feel about 1 Peter 2:21-23 and Luke 9:23-25?

7. From Luke 9:23-25, what is the benefit of being willing to take up your cross and what is the consequence of being unwilling to do so?

8. Read 2 Corinthians 4:10-18. What are the benefits and the end result of sharing in the death of Jesus?

9. Knowing that God may choose to allow suffering and pain to come into our lives, what difference do the promises of Psalm 23:4 and Isaiah 43:2 make to you personally?

Read the corresponding chapter in Holding on to Hope: *Epilogue*

WEEK 8

God's Sovereignty in Suffering

Small Group Discussion Questions

1. If God does not willingly bring affliction or enjoy hurting people, why would he choose to allow suffering to come into our lives (Lamentations 3:22-33)?

2. What difference does that truth make as you struggle with the question of why God would choose to allow hurt to come into your life?

3. Does the fact that God may have allowed a wicked person to hurt you or someone you love make what happened good? Is that the same thing as God using it for good in your life or the lives of others?

4. God was willing to allow wicked men to put Jesus on the cross to accomplish the work of salvation. How does this impact your ability to see that God could use something that could only be described as bad for good in your life?

5. What do you think it means to "take up your cross" (Matthew 10:38)?

6. How have you experienced giving up your life for Christ and finding true life?

7. After studying the book of Job, can you now explain exactly why bad things happen and why the innocent suffer? If not, can you be comfortable with that ambiguity?

8. How does Deuteronomy 29:29 help you with the ambiguity of trying to understand the why of suffering?

Visit

ChristianBookGuides.com

for a discussion guide and other book group
resources for *Holding on to Hope*.

A portion of the proceeds from the sale
of this book goes to the

Hope & Gabriel Guthrie Memorial
Scholarship Fund

benefiting special-needs students at

Christ Presbyterian Academy
2323A Old Hickory Blvd.
Nashville, TN 37214

Donations are welcome